PRAYER

TO

SILENCE

FINANCIAL CRISES

By Tella Olayeri
08023583168

All rights reserved under International Copyright Law. Content may not be reproduced in whole or in part or in any form without the consent of the publisher.

Email; tellaolayeri@gmail.com
Website www.tellaolayeri.com

US Contact
Ruth Jack
14 Milewood Road
Verbank
N.Y.12585
U.S.A. +19176428989

APPRECIATION

I give special appreciation to my wife MRS NGOZI OLAYERI for her assistance in ensuring that this book is published and our children that played around us to encourage us day and night.

Also, this manuscript wouldn't have seen the light of the day, if not for the spiritual encouragement I gathered from my father in the Lord, Dr. D.K. OLUKOYA who served as spiritual mirror that brightens my hope to explore my calling (Evangelism).

We shall all reap our blessings in heaven but the battle to make heaven is not over, until it is won.

PREFACE

Success occurs when talents meet opportunity. Success belongs to those who see and think it. Those who did it are great investors, performers, dynamics, and highly astute leaders who turn things around. They are men and women of destiny, meant for the top, created for impact, configured for excellence, packaged to be distinguished, called to be great and ordained to be celebrated.

This book says it all. It will guide you step by step to wealth creation and how to manage it at old age! It is your birthright to succeed. You are loaded with gold, it is time you develop and harvest. Wasted years and wasted efforts are over.

As a financial combatant, silence financial crisis, build financial discipline that will accelerate you to the top. With the book in your hand, you shall discover deposits of gold and wealth. You shall write off your liabilities and occupy asset based status.

The hurdle is crossed as you pick this book. I say congratulation!

GOOD NEWS!!!

My audiobook is now available. To get one go to acx.com and search **Tella Olayeri**.

Thanks.

PREVIOUS PUBLICATIONS OF THE AUTHOR

1. *Fire for Fire Prayer Book Part 1*
2. *Fire for Fire Prayer Book Part 2*
3. *My Marriage Shall Not Break*
4. *Prayer for Pregnant Women*
5. *Prayer for the Fruit of the Womb*
6. *Children Deliverance*
7. *Prayer for Youths and Teenagers*
8. *Prayer for Singles*
9. *Victory over Satanic House Part 1*
10. *Victory over Satanic House Part 2*
11. *I Shall Excel*
12. *Atomic Prayers that Destroy Witchcraft Powers and Silence Enemies*
13. *Goliath at the Gate of Marriage*
14. *Deliverance from Spirit of Dogs*
15. *Naked Warriors*
16. *Prayer Against Sex in the Dream*
17. *Strange Women! Leave My Husband Alone*
18. *Dangerous Prayer against Strange Women*
19. *630 Acidic Prayer Points*
20. *Power to Retain Job and Excel in Office*
21. *Warfare in the Office*
22. *Command the Year*
23. *Deliverance Prayer for First Born*
24. *800 Deliverance Prayer for First Born Part Two*
25. *Prayer for Good Health and Divine Healing*
26. *Prayer against Untimely Death.*
27. *Dictionary of Dreams*

28. *Prayer to Silence Financial Crises*
29. *My Head is not for Sale*
30. *830 Prophecies for the Head*
31. *874 Prayers to Destroy Destiny Killers*
32. *Prayer after Dream*
33. *Prayer to Locate Helpers and helpers to locate you*
34. *Anointing for Eleventh Hour Help*
35. *100% Confessions and Prophecies to Locate Helpers and helpers to locate you*
36. *Prayer to Remember Dreams*
37. *1010 Dreams and interpretations*
38. *650 Dreams and Interpretation*
39. *.1,000 Prayer Points for Children Breakthrough*
40. *I Am Not Alone*
41. *My Well of Honey shall not dry*
42. *Shake Heaven with Prayer and Praises*
43. *Deliverance Prayers for Middle Born Part One*
44. *800 Deliverance Prayer Points for Middle Born Part Two*
45. *Deliverance Prayers for Last Born Part One*
46. *800 Deliverance Prayer Points for Last Born Part Two*
47. *365 Dreams and Interpretations*
48. *700 Prayers to clear Unemployment Out of your Way*
49. *777 Deliverance Prayers for Healing and Breakthrough*
50. *Bad Dreams Enemies Use to Rob Blessing and the Way Out Part One*
51. *Bad Dreams Enemies Use to Rob Blessing and the Way Out Part Two*
52. *Bad Dreams Enemies Use to Rob Blessing and the Way Out Part Three*

53. 430 Prayer to Cancel Bad Dreams And Overcome Witchcraft Powers Part One
54. 430 Prayers to Claim Good Dreams And Overcome Witchcraft Powers Part Two
55. Command the Night Against 100 types of Witchcraft Arrows
56. Command the Night 30 Days Spiritual Manual Prayer Book
57. Command the Day
58. Command the Night with 90 Decrees And Prophecies
59. Command the Night Deal with Witchcraft Powers and be Set Free
60. Command the Night Against Battles of Life
61. Command the Night against Family Disorder and Marital Attack
62. Command the Night with 370 Prayers Against Deadly Arrows that Bury Destiny
63. Command the Night with 444 Prophetic Prayers to Move from the Valley to Mountain Top
64. Total Body Deliverance
65. Dangerous Decree and Prophecies Part One
66. Dangerous Decree and Prophecies Part Two
67. Prayer to Pray When Debtors Owe You and Refuse to Pay
68. Dreams and Vision and Ways to Understand their Mysterious Meanings Part One
69. Dreams and Vision and Ways to Understand their Mysterious Meanings Part Two
70. Dreams and Vision and Ways to Understand their Mysterious Meanings Part Three
71. Prayer in time of Emergency

72. *Prayer when all seems Lost*
73. *Calling God to silence Witchcraft Powers*
74. *Prayer to Secure Golden Breakthrough Job*
75. *I Fire You Part One*
76. *I Fire You Part Two*
77. *I Fire You Part Three*
78. *Prayer to Make Wealth and Sink Poverty Part One*
79. *Prayer to Make Wealth and Sink Poverty Part Two*
80. *Thunder and Fire Prayers That Scatter Witchcraft Activities*
81. *99 Ways of Unprofitable Wealth*
82. *2000 Super Deliverance Prayers for First Born*
83. *Biblical Prayer Against Sickness and Diseases*
84. *740 Rocket Prayers that Break Satanic Embargo*
85. *Dangerous Prayer that Makes Satan flee and Surrender Your Possession*
86. *Double Fire Double Thunder Prayer Book*
87. *Praying Through Pandemic and Receive Solution*
88. *Prayer To Break The Head Of Dragon*
89. *It Is War! Declare Your Enemies Defeated And Destroy Them*

Table of Contents

SECRET TO SUCCESS 11

STARTING OUT A NEW BUSINESS 25

POWER OF INFORMATION 45

HAVE A FARMER, NOT A HUNTER MENTALITY 53

RUN YOUR BUSINESS WELL 67

AVOID FINANCIAL CRISIS 80

DISCOVER GOLD IN STOCKS 110

GOLD AND WEALTH IN DIET 127

CHAPTER ONE
SECRET TO SUCCESS

Success belongs to those who see and think it. Those who did it are great innovator, performer, dynamics, and highly astute leaders who turn things around. They are men and women of destiny, meant for the top, created for impact, configured for excellence, packaged to be distinguished, called to be great and ordained to be celebrated.

The credential of successful men and women are superb. They make things happen which has never happened before. They respond to the large build-up of expectations and hopes of people. They mend broken dreams, frown at mismanagement and believe in super economic policies, study growth rates of the economy, understand complex issues and deal with conflicting interests as they arise. All these don't just happen, they happen because they assemble the best available materials in human capital and machine to pursue their goal.

When we see successful people, we often assume that they got all the breaks, that they were always in the right place at the right time, that they've never failed or never been rejected even once. If

the truth were known, very few people accomplish anything worthwhile the first time they attempt it.
The secret to success is to do something positive and bring something good out of it. Everyone is born unique and there is something special in every individual. What you need is to discover what you have and develop it. Success in business is best measured by whether you have created something that you can be really proud of and whether you've made a difference for others.

Success is our birth right, and God is the author of success. He created man to succeed and to be fulfilled in life. That some have achieved great success is a proof that others can achieve it as well. Hence, everybody can succeed.

Your chance to succeed lies ahead; it is a matter of whether or not you choose to pursue it. The ladder of success doesn't care who climbs it. Success befriends whosoever fulfils its requirements. Success cares less of stature, colour, height, age, nationality, family background, handicap or sex. Success comes to only those that care to follow its principles.

The fact that success is good and desired by everyone does not mean that success is cheap. It is not. It is you that matters in business. Your effort speaks volume. That some people have advantage is not enough reason to succeed, and that some people have all the disadvantages is not enough reason to fail. What matter is you; not your bank account. Though it is good to be capital based, it is not an end in itself. It is the talent and will in you that matters. Bank account can liquidate anytime, asset in you can't. Let the in-built in you fire investment to explosion. Here you talk of **Steve Jobs** at **Apple, Larry Page** at **Google; Richard Branson** at **Virgin, and Bill Gates** at **Microsoft.**

These great men of our time know success because they love what they enjoy doing, even in the midst of distraction, developing their skills and talents. Business favours people who, when they see a problem, or an injustice, try to do something about it. At such point, you can contact a mentor who has experience in the area you are thinking about entering. Nonetheless, a good mentor is not necessarily someone who is well-known, but rather someone who is leading a rich and enriching life.

To climb ladder of success and get to the top, you must be someone who can dream dreams; have vision and focus, make decision about the direction of your life; break dream into stages and pursue it with determination to succeed. It is when people see your efforts they help. Some people will be touched to help when they see the sacrifices you made. Carry your load at the heaviest side so that helpers may emerge.

People that have no dream would be doomed. White House, the house of power in US wouldn't have had its value, if not for its plan and successful execution. The story may be long, but it was achieved at last.

When **President Thomas Jefferson** (who had submitted a lasting design) moved into the White House in 1801, he began energetically planning additions, but these were not finished until after the mansion was partly burnt by the British during the war of 1812. It was painted white for the first time under **James Madison**, filled with indoor plumbing by **Andrew Jackson** and given the official designation; **White House** by **Theodore Roosevelt.**

The White House contains 54 major rooms including porticos and measures 168 feet in length by 152 feet in width. It is surrounded by more than 18 acres of landscaped lawns and gardens.

The White House is normally open from 10am to 12:00noon Tuesday to Saturday and from 10am to 2pm in the summer. Only the public rooms on the ground floor and state floor may be visited. As everyone knows, it is the residence of US President.

If not for the bold step taken by Jefferson, the story of White House may be different today. People who approach things with order, common sense, consistency and persistence are always found at the top of the ladder of success. Success seems to be connected with action. Men and women of success keep moving. They make mistakes, but don't quit. The key to success is focus and perseverance.

Whatever dream you have pursue it. Don't delay till tomorrow, when to start is now. Pursue your dream with vigour, dedication and prayer. The success recorded in science and technology in the world today, is as result of some peoples' dream. They dream BIG and achieve BIG. Your dream can be a business dream, a career dream, a marriage dream, a project dream, a training dream or academic dream.

Develop that in built success in you. Invention is in built. Don't look down on yourself or others. When you hear of what great inventors do, you may marvel, but there is great stuff in them. The people who make technological wonders possible are often cultural and social misfits. They are the kind of people our society disdain. Let's take **Einstein, Edison** and **Shannon** as example.

Einstein, who is widely acclaimed as the brightest mind of the 20th century, indulged in eccentricities. For instance, he reportedly would pick up cigarette butts from the streets, retrieved the tobacco for his pipe and smoked while riding his bicycle carefree like a boy.

Edison the inventor was known for going for days without taking a birth. The resulting body odour made him not too pleasant to be around. He routinely put in 16-hour workdays, sometimes catching a nap by stretching out under a table. His understanding wife had to have a bed installed in his workplace.

Shannon, whose mathematical theory of information was the impetus of our digital age, was a shy introvert who shunned social interactions, even with his colleagues at the Bells Labs. The result was, he developed computer that could play chess.

Fire the motivation in you for success, rather than kill your appetite spending time to worry or wait an easy life. Pursue activities and tasks with all sense of commitment. Spend time, money, energy and resource on the job that gives you maximum profit.

Two people are involved in determining your success in life; you, and of course God. Put all efforts in whatever you do as God never design our lives for struggles and failures. Don't look around to blame your background, lack of education, the government, leader, witchcraft or wizards for your failure. Being creative is not anybody's birthright.

Everybody is bound to creative in whatever situation or environment they find themselves. You are in a race which you must win. In all races several people are usually at the starting line, but it is only three people that qualify for prices, the first, the second and the third position. For you to excel, improve on anything that brings you income. By this, you shall climb the ladder and occupy space at the top, where fresh breeze abound.

Above all, we should look at our **innate ability**. We all have one; that is what stands you out in the midst of a crowd. When you find it, acquire skills to polish the talent. You must relate your talent to the needs in the society and try to meet those needs. As a person, you may not be an employee rather you can be an employer of labour.

In the search for success many found themselves in captivity called **brain drain**. Pharaoh did not go for military expedition to capture Israel; they walk into his enclaves and became slaves that built pyramids. When you remove first letters from brain and drain, you have rain-rain. Hence, brain-drain can lead to rain-rain of unemployment, poverty, ignorance etc if it is not well managed. **William Shakespeare** (1564-1616) in his book **Julius Caesar** said in Act 1 scene 3, Line 101: **Casca**: "So every bondman in his own hands bears the power to cancel his captivity"

Oh yes, everyone bears in his hand the means to end self-imposed, self-volunteered captivity and neo-colonial slavery. But before you can escape flood of poverty, you must pray against powers or government that may despotically, uninspiringly and unjustifiably nail your ambition. Lest we forget what Kwamme Nkrumah of Ghana said in his book "Dark days in Ghana"; that a country under a military regime is a country under internal colonialism.

I pray you shall not be under bondage that will stagnate your life. Amen.

AVOID WRONG LADDER OF LIFE

There are people that occupy wrong ladder of life. It is good to understand the career you pick. It is impossible to succeed in a profession that is not meant for you. The reason is that square peg won't fit in round hole. It would have been different if you channel your energy into career that opens door of success.

Really, it may take a number of years to realize that you made a mistake in choosing a career, but you must address it as fast as possible, so that you don't gnash your teeth day in day out. It is not until you disengage in wrong venture before you can discover the gold in you.

PRAYER TO SILENCE FINANCIAL CRISES

There are numerous warning signs you can look out for in order to determine if you have erred when you decided what profession or job you would spend your time doing. Such signs can be summarized as follows: -

When you lack pride in your career. This includes, unwillingness to discuss your career with people, or you are fed up at work every day.

When you lack passion or commitment of what you do; not seeing good future in your job, not working with right people or not doing what you are good at.

When you are not connected to the company's vision or goal

When you drag yourself to work every day, only to give one excuse or the other, to go to hospital or go for one burial occasion or so.

When you aren't good at your work, only to make one mistake or the other every day, it suggests you are on a wrong career.

When you go in late to office but leave early, it suggests you are not motivated in your work, or you have very little to do, or you don't care to complete your work.

When you don't feel challenged with what you do, it suggests you should look for a better career that can bring your strength to it.

When you look for ways to keep you busy, know that your career is not challenging and so, you need more demanding career.

Once you discover that your business or career is not fruitful and you have used every human effort possible it is advisable to look for best opportunity cost benefit. It is a disaster to pump resources and energy in a business that records failure after failure. There are people who belief in the popular saying, "Winners never quit and quitters never win, failure is not an option". I advise, quit bad business or career when occasion demands.

The commonest reason why people refuse to quit is the pain of letting go after so much time and money have been invested in getting things work. "The sacrifices, progress made so far and lessons learnt are just too much or hard to relinquish" so they say. But then, you don't need to bury yourself in problems, rather take stock of your life and have a break, discuss issues with reliable friends or your bank, and choose best options available on the table.

I say good luck.

PRAYER TO SILENCE FINANCIAL CRISES

PRAYER POINTS

1. Lord Jesus, give me power to think, see and achieve success in the name of Jesus.

2. Secret to success appear, occupy my life in the name of Jesus.

3. Every barrier between me and success scatter in the name of Jesus.

4. O Lord, empower me to occupy ladder of success until I get to the top in the name of Jesus.

5. Power to discover, what is in me appear in the name of Jesus.

6. Success is my birth right I claim it by fire in the name of Jesus.

7. I shall not be a slave to others in the name of Jesus.

8. I march from minimum level to maximum level of greatness in the name of Jesus.

9. Any witchcraft re-arrangement for my sake, scatter in the name of Jesus.

10. My helpers locate and help me in the name of Jesus.

11. I fire back, every arrow of failure fired against me in the name of Jesus.

12. Agony of failure, quit my life and die in the name of Jesus.

13. Any power, assign to keep me in the wrong position of life die in the name of Jesus.

14. Family idol pulling me down from the ladder of success die in the name of Jesus.

15. Mighty hand of God, take me to my Promised Land in the name of Jesus.

16. I shall not experience disgrace in my calling or career in the name of Jesus.

17. Wasters of destiny assign to waste me be wasted in the name of Jesus.

18. Satanic pregnancy assign to bear spiritual children of failure for me be aborted in the name of Jesus.

19. My father and my God give me supernatural knowledge above my contemporaries in the name of Jesus.

20. O Lord, open my eyes to deep things that will elevate me in the name of Jesus.

PRAYER TO SILENCE FINANCIAL CRISES

21. Every reinforcement, against my success, die in the name of Jesus.

22. I render powerless every power assign against my breakthrough in the name of Jesus.

23. Terrors assign against my success, die, in the name of Jesus.

24. Every foundational curse, against my success, break in the name of Jesus.

25. Opposition against my success, scatter in the name of Jesus.

26. Tragedy of failure waiting me at the point of success be nullified in the name of Jesus.

27. Spirit of demotion assign to attack and demote me die in the name of Jesus.

28. Thou valley assign to swallow my success, expire in my life, in the name of Jesus

29. Bondage of debt in my life, break, in the name of Jesus.

30. Cloud of uncertainty upon my life, clear away, in the name of Jesus.

31. Holy Spirit pilot my life to level of success in the name of Jesus.

32. Every verdict of darkness against my success scatter in the name of Jesus.

33. Any power assign to break the ladder of my success, die, in the name of Jesus.

34. Milk and honey of success locate me by fire in the name of Jesus.

CHAPTER TWO

STARTING OUT A NEW BUSINESS

The starting point of a business is tasking hard no matter your bravery. To start a business, you are either into a paid employment, trying to quit for entrepreneurship, unemployed or you dim it fit to start something doing after school.

Before you dream of one or start it, many were into it. Many failed while others succeeded. The sun that shines today is the sun that shone when your father was born, and will still be shining when your last grandchild shall pass away. The same sun smites many, and save others. I pray that the sun shall not smite you. Amen

The fact remains that as good as the plan to start one may be, many who tried to execute one failed miserably for one reason or the other. It is good to have great idea, it is another to establish and make it fruitful. It takes more than having an idea. Whatever the cloud, dark, threatening or inviting, you must be prepared to take certain steps, failure to do so, may reduce your chances of achieving your goal.

Why struggle for existence when goldmines are all around you. Despite time and energy exerted, many failed to make it to the top. Why, because they failed to learn the laws that govern the building of wealth. There are rules to follow before you can be a gold digger, a wealth builder and a guru entrepreneur. Let's discuss rules that open one's way to palace of wealth below.

First thing is, you must **be qualified** to run the race of entrepreneurship. As good as the idea of being your own boss is, not many are capable of running or becoming successful entrepreneur. You must be loaded as a person in term of discipline, hard work, self-confidence, credibility, good inter personal skill etc. The last in this series entail's you have excellent communication, human and time management skill. Really, some of the skills required to run a business can be acquired or improved upon while on the field, but then, starting without the required skills would be a costly mistake. It is therefore necessary to qualify.

Another; is to **prepare properly** for the task ahead. Unpreparedness is a license to crisis. Preparation is the bed rock of business. You mustn't rush at doing things when you plan to be an entrepreneur. Take all the time needed to carry out your survey and prepare properly. Survey and research will determine whether you need additional preparations.

Questions that may arise include, are there skills I require to run the business that I don't have? Am I really ready to start a business? Will I be able to put in the required hours? Do I need to wait for a year or more to resolve some issues in the family? You may miss it all and not discover gold or build wealth if you fail to prepare before you go into business.

Another point to note is to **be sure of what you want to do**. Many are fond of sailing in the sea of uncertainty, calling it progress. Hence, you must be sure about what you want to do, how to go about it and why you want to start the business. When you are armed this way, it becomes easy to handle challenges and go through issues without relenting.

Don't be afraid of emergency situations. When it comes God shall arise concerning your situation. Does your situation need emergency to turn things around for good? If yes is your answer, there is no other two ways to it than to have my book titled **32 EMERGENCY TELEPHONE CALLS OF GOD**. It shall address every emergency situation you face. You can only discover gold and build wealth when you address emergency situations you face. This book is a must for you.

Another thing is to **come up with a great concept**. Before you conclude to start a business or career, first think of a concept, product or service that will generate a steady stream of income. It is recommended that you start out with a business that you are passionate and knowledgeable about.

This reminds me of a building expert who pursued his vision, even to the grave! It is about the construction of **Brooklyn Bridge**, which **links Brooklyn to Manhattan Island**, one of the most famous bridges in the world. At the time it was first conceived in 1883, however, bridge building experts throughout the world told the designer, a creative engineer by the name of **John Roebling** that his idea wouldn't work.

Roebling convinced his son Washington, who was also an engineer that his idea would work. They developed the concept, resolved the problems others forecasted, and hired a crew to build the bridge.
After a few month of building a disaster occurred, that took the life of John Roebling and several others injured. His son Washington was a bit lucky as he was badly injured unable to talk or walk! At this point everybody lost hope, that the bridge couldn't be completed.

But Washington proved them wrong as he could still think, and with burning desire to see the bridge finished. As he laid in the bed, he ordered his wife to be by his side. Whenever the engineers come, he would use one finger to tap out in code on his wife's arm what he wanted to tell them. He tapped out his instructions for 13years until the bridge was built. The concept of his father came to fruitiness, even after his death. It is as if Washington borrowed a leaf from the statement of **Theodore Roosevelt** when he said, "Do what you can, with what you have, where you are".

One important point is to **create a great business plan.** No matter the amount of support, help, expertise and funds at your disposal, without a great business plan; you may not succeed in setting up a good business.

Your business plan is supposed to be the blueprint or guide to everything you do regarding the business. It contains everything from your goal or vision, to the nature of product or service you want to provide, among other things. Business plan is the commercial police and tutor that direct the pendulum of an organization.

Another vital point is to **determine and source for funds** to form your capital. The best option to start business is to raise the capital on your own. It is only when this is not enough you can look for it elsewhere. Save even a little and avoid unnecessary leakage. Beware of little expenses as a small leak may sink a ship. No matter how big a balloon is, a single pin is all it takes to deflate it. Brethren, a part of all you earn is yours to keep. It should be not less than a tenth no matter how little you earn. It can be as much more as you can afford. Pay yourself first and do not buy what you don't need.

You need money to start business. To secure money is one thing another is to manage it well. Many entrepreneurs make the mistake of thinking that a successful business is well to the amount of money available for the business. But business floated with millions of cash has gone on to fail, while those established with thousands of cash have grown to become billion in assets and profit.

To realize gold in business, in sourcing funds, it is important you go to right sources. As a startup it is better off to depend on friends and relatives, or depend on personal savings. The mistake of many people is that they turn to banks and borrow huge sums at high interest rates, hoping that they would break even in a short while and pay off the loans. But the reality is that because of the interest rates, they find themselves using all their profits to service the loans, with little left to grow the business.

If ever you need a **bank loan**, it is good you **study the terms and conditions well**. Apart from collateral interest payable; tenor Bank offer Letters always include a set of "Other Terms and Conditions" "OTC" Most fail to read these additional conditions and usually result in the bank having enormous powers over your business and determining what it can do in times of dispute.

Another gray area with bank is that you can ask your bank for a *moratorium*. A moratorium is simply a bank permission to a borrower to suspend repayment of principal for a period of time, because some businesses require time to start making money.

Banks recognize that and will often allow borrowers a period of grace (one month, three month, one year etc.) where they only pay interest and resume paying interest and principal at the end of the moratorium. That way the business can use the extra cash to invest in the business. The biggest threat to business is not default to pay your loan interest but your **Debt Service Coverage Ratio.** Your **DSCR** is simply about cash flow compatibility. The cash you generate must be able to cover the repayment of your loans and interest after you deduct your operating cost. If this ratio is less than one, then you are more likely to default and face the wrath of the bank.

Make sure you identify the right bank that understands your business and your goals, so that you may make gold in business and build wealth.

Another vital step to discover gold in business and build wealth is to **draw up a budget** for the business. You must not rely on assumption of what to spend or finance a business. For a business to utilize scarce funds effectively, it is better operated on a budget. As such, it is good you draw up budgets for your business. You can do this better when you carry out research or market surveys in respect of the business in mind.

Concentrate and bring out facts and figures that will guide you. It is by so doing, you will be sure of what you want to do, how to do it and when to start or do it.

Market research enables your plan and develops your idea. It also determines many other things such as where to get your needed items from and where to set up your business etc. One most important thing research can help you achieve is to know your market. It will enable you know if your product or service is needed at all.

From research you will know who are your competitors, their strength and weaknesses as well; and how you can win customers and build your market share. The only certain means of success is to render more and better services than is expected. The person who gets ahead is the one who does more than is necessary and keeps on doing it.

Another vital step to take as an investor or an entrepreneur is to **seek professional help.** One of the biggest mistakes shareholders, investors or entrepreneur make is to ignore professional helps. The fact is, we don't like to pay for services, but like to pay for physical goods that we can see. We believe professionals are people that are just trying to make money for themselves.

As an investor you need advice of professionals. Ignoring professional advice and studies can be severe leading to loss of investment. You may want to avoid them because it may cost you, but the cost of doing everything by yourself is even more costly. In starting your own business, you need to talk to lawyers, financial or investment experts, accountants etc. They will not only guide or advice you on what you need to be done, they will help it done. For instance, in registering your business, and draw up employee contracts you need the service of a lawyer. Similarly, an investment expert or financial adviser will tell you if your business plan is too risky or overly speculative. You can get a successful entrepreneur to be your mentor as well.

To achieve an enabling robust business, you need to get a **strategic office.** The nature of the business you want to do and the location of your targeted customer base are some of the things you have to take into consideration in citing your office or workplace. Whether you are working from home or renting an office, be sure that your workspace is designed to enable you work effectively and efficiently. If you are running an e-commerce business, then you must ensure that your website is designed properly or professionally. Your website represents your office.

When you start a business have it at the back of your mind that one day you may **expand or diversify to other areas**. A common mistake investors make is that when they make an investment that turn out great, they hold on to it. To them, it is tested and trusted, a sure bet. They no longer heed warning signs and are likely to be caught napping when the investment goes bad. The fact is that what is a good investment today is not guaranteed to remain that way tomorrow. Let's take this case study as an example.

In the early 1900s, when cotton was "King" the boll weevil crossed over from Mexico to the United States and destroyed the cotton plants. Farmers were forced to grow a variety of crops, as they were hit by unexpected disaster. They went for soybeans and peanuts as a test run and may be last hope. The step they took paid off, many more farmers became prosperous than in the days when the only crop grown was cotton.

The people of enterprise, Alabama, were so grateful for what had occurred that, in 1910 they erected a monument to boll weevil. The power of diversification favoured them. When they turned from the single crop system to diversified farming, they became wealthier. The inscription on the monument read; "In profound appreciating of the boll weevil and what it has done to herald prosperity"!

Next, is to **be creative and plan for the future**. In this time of situational challenges like weather change, uprisings here and there, ecological threats, terrorism, probable economic meltdown etc, every entrepreneur must plan well and read into the future. By this, you must not only interview or take counsels from professionals, but ensure that your business is ahead of the competition and the times.

To achieve this, it is important that you **predict and react to possible trends in the future.** You have to reinvent your business constantly to beat market challenges. Hence, you have to plan for the growth of the business and the challenges that may come with it. Also, you have to ensure that your business can adapt to changing times and economic challenges.

Another important area to look into when starting a new business is to **exhibit undefeatable determination**. Learn to fight the battle and push on; in the word of Sir Winston Churchill, "Never, never, never, never give up" The fact remains, ninety percent of all those who fail are not actually defeated. They simply quit. They fail because; they quickly forgot there is always light at the end of the tunnel.

PRAYER TO SILENCE FINANCIAL CRISES

The story was told of **Marshall Field** who build a towering monument on the ashes of his wealth. How did it happen? Here is the story.

There happened to be a great Chicago fire disaster some years back. The morning after the tragic fire, a group of merchants stood on the state street, looking at the smoking remains of what had been their stores. Everyone lost everything. There was an emergency conference to decide on what next to do, either to rebuild or leave Chicago and start over in a more promising section of the country. They reached a decision, all except one to leave Chicago; Marshall Field.

This man built a merchant aggressive mind. He refused to listen to reasons of others to quit. He eventually became a "Prophet of the day when he exclaimed, in the face of everyone present, "Gentlemen, on that very spot I will build the world's greatest store, no matter how many times it may burn down"

This incidence took place a long time ago. The store was rebuilt. It stands there today as a towering monument to the power of determination.

It is a testimony of don't quit, even in the face of defeat.

A vital step to take in a startup business is to invest in **financial education.** Most of our financial education or lack of it comes from home, school, places of worship, place of work and peer group. At times mostly when we were young, we got the idea from our parents, whether they are literate or otherwise. It is all about the way they spoke about money and the way we saw them handle money.

The fact remains, if you want to stay in business, you must know how to handle money. Not this day, when resources are limited and human needs are insatiable. When limited resources meet insatiable needs, the result is a constant state of lack. A good entrepreneur should learn to invest for profit and enjoy the fruit of his investment.

Education plays good role in financial literacy but it is not an end in itself. Many attributes like discipline, dedication, market forecast etc. must be added to it. At times, you see those who are not educated setting up business, doing well and employ educated people. The fact remains, first class graduates and PhD holders work for folks who drop out of school or never went beyond first degree. This buttress the fact, that academic performance is not an indicator of success in life.

There are three broad types of education namely, academic, professional and financial education. All are important, if you want to succeed in every aspect of business. But then, without financial education, an individual and his money soon part ways. It is on record, many who were millionaires in years back went into liquidation due to lack of financial literacy.

When you are financially illiterate, you make poor financial decisions and sentence yourself to a lifetime financial struggle. To avoid this, invest in yourself, especially financial education. As you become better educated, you are loaded to make better investment decision which results in better returns on investment.

Doing all we enumerated earlier, shall enable you build solid business financial base with an exploring financial plan. The latter, financial plan brings into view the sales and costs plan for a business and how cash will flow in and out of the business at a particular point in time. It also reveals the profitability potential of a business, informing ahead of time the possible profits or losses over a period of time.

Financial planning doesn't mean record keeping alone, it goes far and wide. For example, it entails discovery of whether the product you want to sell is okay for the amount of money you want to put into the business. If you fail or incur debt, you may end up thinking whether witches and wizards are after you. This is not so, it is because you lack financial plan.

With all the humanly principles you may adopt **support your business in prayer**. It is prayer that brings protective hands of God upon a business for blessings and breakthroughs. Prayer silences wicked advancement against a business. It makes you loaded with wisdom to operate an adventure that brings BIG DREAMS into perfection.

You need to pray fire prayers to excel in life. This can be done when you open your mouth wide and ask God what you want and what you reject.
I advise we go into session of prayer. Now let's pray.

PRAYER POINTS

1. Sun of breakthrough, shine upon my business in the name of Jesus

PRAYER TO SILENCE FINANCIAL CRISES

2. Ideas that will lead to fruitfulness manifest in my life in the name of Jesus

3. Goldmines destined to promote my cause, appear and promote me in the name of Jesus

4. Lord Jesus, turn me to digger and builder of wealth in the name of Jesus. I am loaded with tools to succeed in the name of Jesus

5. Every obstacle standing between me and my business clear away in the name of Jesus.

6. Favour of God, locate me by fire in the name of Jesus

7. Afflictions that choke breakthrough, my life is not your candidate die, in the name of Jesus.

8. My business, receive fire of deliverance in the name of Jesus

9. Any cursed land assign to swallow my wealth, you shall fail in the name of Jesus

10. I shall not carry out satanic errands in the place of my business in the name of Jesus

11. Holy Spirit, give me right direction to succeed in life in the name of Jesus

12Spirit of failure, quit my life, in the name of Jesus

13. I pronounce destruction upon powers challenging my success in the name of Jesus

14. I shall not mortgage my business in the name of Jesus

15. Every arrow of sickness fired against me, in other to disrupt my business back fire in the name of Jesus

16. My business plan shall not be replaced by plans of darkness in the name of Jesus

17. Every instrument assign against my business die in the name of Jesus

18. Every satanic money assign to scatter my business, you are a failure, die in name of Jesus.

19. Poverty shall not swallow my business in the name of Jesus.

PRAYER TO SILENCE FINANCIAL CRISES

20. Dark parasites eating my business die in the name of Jesus

21. Evil rain falling on my business, stop by fire in the name of Jesus

22. Witchcraft covenant troubling my business, break in the name of Jesus

23. Every debt recorded against me in the spirit, be cancelled by the blood of Jesus

24. Heavenly budget take over my business in the name of Jesus

25. Witchcraft research against my business, scatter in the name of Jesus

26. Satanic wisdom to derail me, scatter, in the name of Jesus

27. Every dark contractor assign to take over my business die in the name of Jesus

28. I shall not locate my business at the junction of disappointment in the name of Jesus

29. Every dark padlock fashioned against my business break to pieces in the name of Jesus

30. Thou light of God, shine upon my business in the name of Jesus

31. Any power assign to turn my business promises to dung hill die in the name of Jesus

32. Thou gate of bankruptcy holding my business to nothing, break to pieces, in the name of Jesus

33. Holy Ghost Fire, electrocute witchcraft powers in my business in the name of Jesus.

CHAPTER THREE
POWER OF INFORMATION

Information is the mainstay of business going concern. Information comes in form of data and words of mouth. With information we plan, organize and control our business. Business information kept includes customer details, prices, stock levels, business agreements etc. For an entrepreneur to discover gold and build wealth in what he does, information is paramount. It is therefore necessary to protect vital business information in other to grow and excel. A business that will stand test of time must be well nurtured, and also provided with right watering and pruning. In protecting business data, it helps to restrict access to sensitive records which outsiders may not gain access to.

In coming together to build wealth, information is vital. To run a business and improve on it depends on information gathering. If you have millions of dollars without adequate human and technical information, your money may disappear. It is therefore good to equip yourself with information that will make you dig gold and build wealth.

Information may be stored in **personal computers**, and or, **auto backups** like hard discs and flash drives. As a result of transformation from a paper based system to electronics, huge file cabinets have largely disappeared. Information is stored for security and to get it when needed. When stored this way, we tend to consider ourselves immune to losses. But this is not often so, because when flood or fire disaster occur we may lose them all. You can imagine losing data and information of debtors running to millions of money. If such happens, your debtors may deny ever owing you, or avoid you. This is one reason you should recognize the benefits of information storage.

Another reason for information storage and safety is that it checks corrupt activities of staff and it saves cost. Once transactions are done on the computer, before it can be edited, it might need authorization from the boss or a superior, and that might deter some people from corrupt acts. This act alone saves an entrepreneur from unexpected fold up as "caterpillar and cankerworms" mouths are sealed.

PRAYER TO SILENCE FINANCIAL CRISES

This day gold and wealth are created by adopting **online back up**. Beside this, there are some companies that handle data backup for business by keeping very sensitive information for clients. When you do, in the time your data get corrupted or damaged, or you have software problems, you can recover your data online. There are websites online that can help people to store data free or at minimal cost.

For confidence, I will say you shouldn't be carried away with fear of hackers as your information may not be useful to any other person other than you. So when you back it up online and a hacker gains access to it, you have nothing to lose. If you are not satisfied this way, you can have backup for very sensitive information which you don't want anyone else gain access to and keep it at the end of business activities each day.

Thank God, there is now breakthrough in information recovery as a result of technology. Gone are the days when entrepreneurs panic as a result of lost information due to virus or damage. A lot of companies folded up or have serious challenges because they couldn't recover lost data. They depend so much on their software and auto backup, only for the system to crash or get damaged.

This day, the story has changed. **When hard disc is physically damaged**, a combination of software can be used to retrieve information stored on it. Hence, if your computer or removable device gets corrupted and you can access information stored on it, there is no need to panic. What to do is, look for a data recovery company and tell them your problem for solution at a moderate fee. When you are through and get your data back, it pays far above service charge you pay. Imagine paying N50,000 to recover information that worth 500 million naira!

There is another information power house used to build wealth. It is called **social capital.** It is used to broaden streams of customers that build Business Empire. What do we mean by social capital? it is the number of people that you have direct relationship and access with via any of the social media like e-mail, face book, You tube, etc. and mobile phone contacts.

PRAYER TO SILENCE FINANCIAL CRISES

Your head is loaded with power and information. It is an engine room for gold. The gold in you can be found in the head because it is the reasoning reservoir of the body. There are power points for the head you need to discover and know. They help to reshape destiny for bounty of gold. This can be found in my book titled **30 POWER POINTS FOR THE HEAD.** You need this book, for a quick turnaround in your life. Prayer points in this book can change your life. The prayer points are wonderful, and violent against evil parades against your destiny. Go for it.

I pray your life shall not remain the same but shall move forward by fire Amen. God bless you. Let's go into the act of prayer.

PRAYER POINTS

1. Any power assign to turn my business upside down die in the name of Jesus

2. Messenger of darkness on assignment against my business die on your way in the name of Jesus

3. Every contrary information against my business be nullified in the name of Jesus

4. Every burial assign to misrepresent my business in the spirit die in the name of Jesus

5. Any power assign to extinguish the lamp of my business die in the name of Jesus

6. Every chain of darkness assign to chain my business down break in the name of Jesus

7. I speak against distress calls in respect of my business in the name of Jesus

8. Evil propaganda against my business backfire in the name of Jesus

9. Lord, move me to position of success in the name of Jesus

10. Any power assign to turn my success to failure meet double failure in the name of Jesus

11. Plantation of failure in my business, die to your root in the name of Jesus

12. Those that take pleasure in evil to harm me, shall fail in the name of Jesus

13. Dark grave in my business premises, disappear in the name of Jesus

PRAYER TO SILENCE FINANCIAL CRISES

14. Enemies of my soul, turn back in disgrace in the name of Jesus

15. Lord, spread your hand of protection upon my business in the name of Jesus

16. Every strange hand spread upon my business wither in the name of Jesus

17. I shall not end my business in tears and sorrow in the name of Jesus

18. Strange lion at the door step of my business premises die in the name of Jesus

19. Any power assigned to naked me die in the name of Jesus

20. Lord, strike the jaws of the enemy, break their teeth by fire in the name of Jesus

21. My glory shall not turn to shame in the name of Jesus

22. Every gang up assign to shatter my hope, scatter in the name of Jesus

23. Holy Ghost, silence the voice of the enemy in the name of Jesus

24. Enemies of my business, meet double failure in the name of Jesus

25. Hard work of the enemy, against my business scatter in the name of Jesus

26. Affliction shall not take over my business in the name of Jesus

27. Every curse pronounced against my business backfire in the name of Jesus

28. Every enemy occupying my business, I unsit you by fire in the name of Jesus

29. Dark adverts against my business, backfire and disgrace your sponsors in the name of Jesus.

CHAPTER FOUR

HAVE A FARMER, NOT A HUNTER MENTALITY

"Once when Jacob was cooking some stew, Esau came in from the open country, famished. He said to Jacob, "Quick, let me have some of that red stew! I'm famished!" Genesis 25:29.

This is a story in the Bible we are all familiar with. It is a story of Esau and Jacob. While Esau is noted for hunting, Jacob stayed back at home. The story of the twin changed, when the senior; Esau, sold his birthright for a plate of porridge. He came back from hunting hungry while his brother who prepared porridge gave him a plate in exchange for his birthright. Esau succumbed to Jacob's request, and eventually lost his birthright as first born to receive blessings, to give command and be honoured.

What does being a farmer or a hunter needs to do with business, or better, to discover gold and build wealth? The answer is, there is a strong link and a difference to be a farmer or a hunter. Before we go in depth let's look at who a hunter is and who is qualified to be called a farmer.

A hunter goes to bush either in the day (day time work) or at night (night shift) to look for animals; killing animal is his business for survival. He kills to eat and make little savings for the raining day. The fact is, he hardly has enough animals to kill and eat, and same time sells to keep the funds. At times he goes far into the forest (doing extra labour), yet he may not see animal to kill. The bottom line is, his income is a function of how many animals he is able to kill and carry home. As a result of inability to kill animals every time he went on hunting, he lives one day at a time without much to save for the future. This is the type of life Esau found himself as a hunter. He sold his birthright the day he couldn't find animal to kill. There is nothing in hand to use as exchange for the porridge. The only option left, which Jacob grabbed, was his birthright.

The next question is who is a farmer? A farmer is a person that grows his own animals. He invests in animals like chicken, cow, goats, rabbits, honey bees, sheep, birds etc. The striking difference between him and a hunter is, he owns the animals. He doesn't go hunting, like his friend who is a hunter. Since his animals are accessible and available, he doesn't run out of animals because he rears them. All he needs to do is walk to where they are kept, point out which is needed, and his workers will do the rest. He is able to this on and on because the adults among his animals give birth and the population grows beyond expectation. He is referred to as a gentleman, because he doesn't run after the animals in hot pursuit, risking injuries or health. He is ever robust and good looking. He is a complete gentleman.

You may be at a cross road and ask, what correlation has a farmer or hunter with business or money matters? The relationship is, the farmer and hunter are entrepreneurs in a different way. The hunter works for money while the farmer has money to work for him. The animal is money in this instance; the gun is the educational and professional qualification and work experience for hunting, while the farmer applies command and directives; having enough experience and academic qualifications.

The hunter is never at rest. He leaves home early each day struggling to catch bus or train to work for money, while the farmer grows money in his backyard or at a distance he has access to control. There, money works for him. He expands and adds value to his business. He doesn't only discover gold, but build more wealth with the gold at his disposal. The outstanding difference is, the hunter runs after money while money runs after the farmer. The farmer has opportunity to think and do more networking than his counterpart the hunter, whose expansion is limited. Hence, the farmer gets richer and richer while the hunter struggles to lift his head above water.

Who can be liken to a farmer? They are business owners and investors. They own the assets, both current and fixed assets and put people in charge. They put money to work, and allow their money to grow to generate better returns that gives room to expansion. They encourage diversification in business, monitor it and experience multiple streams of income.

On the other hand, the acts and behavior of a hunter is different. He can be compared to employees in companies and or small business owners. They work hard, toil day and night but never have enough to save for the raining day. As a result, they don't have money that works for them. When they receive salary, wage etc, it is not enough to cater for the home. They live from hand to mouth, no saving after salary, and where little saving exist, it soon flies away.

From this analysis, we can see that many fall victim of being a hunter because they sold their birth right to employers; working for peanuts every month of the year. They are talented but not aggressive enough to bring theirs to manifestation. They have big dreams before they go for employment but never pursue dreams that will make them big, that may raise them from hunter hood to farmer hood. They keep postponing use of what God deposited in them. Their heart is full of fear. Whenever they hear of retrenchment or down size of workforce at work they felt bad and defeated in stroke or illness. Such are the pills swallowed by hunters!

What then can one do to move from being a hunter to be a farmer? The answer can be found in the attitude of Esau who sold his birth right to his junior called Jacob. Esau realized his folly, though late. He changed his reasoning and move from being a hunter to become a farmer. The bible made us to understand, he stopped hunting and started farming and become very wealthy. When Jacob was returning home and heard Esau was coming, he feared. Really, Esau didn't hurt his brother or think evil against Jacob, because he is well to do. His statuses have changed. He is no more a hungry hunter, but a rich farmer.

The question is, who knows what may have happened if Esau was still in his hunting garment and state? He may have called for the head of his brother, and if he failed, Jacob may give him a number of animals that will appease his brother who might even surrender his wives to Jacob as well! Esau changed gear and became far better in animals as a farmer.

To be a hunter (working for someone) is not a crime or an end in itself. It doesn't mean that every employee or small scale business man is a hunter. You can change your status little by little by saving and investing what you have in shares or buy landed properties. Shares may fall during economic meltdown, landed properties increase in value. To improve, you will give a thought for multiple streams of income. Hence you can be a mixture of both, partly a hunter and a farmer.

Another thing is, **you must not consume your way to wealth**. You must not eat the seed for planting. Once you do, harvest is remote. The farmer has to wait for the herd to grow and mature before he starts to 'point and kill'. If he is impatient, he will close down business.

Your future is being created today by your current thoughts and actions. Your financial situation today is a direct consequence of financial decision you took in the past. You created your current financial circumstances as a result of your past financial tact.

You must learn how to **handle well, every money that comes your way**. Money is a good servant but a cruel taskmaster. If you do not master money, money will master you. If you do not work for money, you will end up having to work for money. If you look at money as a seed, you will plant it for a harvest and get more in return. But, when you look at every money that comes your way as harvest, and spend all, you will remain poor. Gold will be far from you.

You must think of multiplier effects in other to secure financial independence. When you have money work for you, you don't push around. You negotiate from a position of strength. Every naira, pound, dollar that comes your way is a potential employee, if you choose yourself as master of money. Here money becomes your employee.

When you start to look at every naira that comes your way as an employee, and keep gathering it, it soon forms an army, working hard and bringing more employees into the fold. If they keep adding and working hard and long enough, your army can grow to the extent of providing for your needs without you having to work.

Let every money coins or note, be of value to you, no matter how small. You can start small and allowing it to build up. When you look at every naira note that comes into your hands as part of your ticket to freedom, you will treat it with more respect. Despise no small amount. Do not disrespect small denominations. They add up to form financial empire. People that respect every denomination grow wealthier. Imagine you keep a piggy bank, from January to December every year, open it and you will be amazed of what you will find! Pay in your dividend cheques no matter how small. Don't feel ashamed to pay in small amount into your account. To save five dollars is great, to save one pound is wonderful, to save #850 less than #1,000 is marvelous! It will swell up your account, little by little! You will discover more gold and build further wealth when you utilize the little you have well.

To discover gold and build wealth you need to speak powerful prophecies unto your head. To achieve this, I endure you buy my book titled **830 PROPHECIES FOR THE HEAD.** When you prophesy good prophecies into your head, heaven will open, angels will arise for your sake, wonders will follow and you shall receive heavenly blessings. This is what this book stands for. Go for it and experience wonders of gold!

Build your mind set if you want to move ahead financially. Build a farmer mentally by investing than build a hunter mentality by consuming what you have rather than invest. If you have been living Esau life change for better. If you live a Jacob life style, who got many herd from his in-law after serving him for fourteen years, better for you. Your service to your present employer was a replica of Jacob's stewardship to his in-law. His investment never close down, rather it multiplied. His name was changed from Jacob to Israel and became father of nation. The prophecy God had for Abraham, came to pass in the life of Jacob, who born twelve children that represents the twelve tribes of Israel. Jacob was a farmer indeed.

I pray your name shall change from Hunter to Farmer! You shall multiply in investment, income and in glory, in the name of Jesus. Amen
Now let's pray

PRAYER POINTS.

1. I shall not sell my destiny to the enemy in the name of Jesus

2. Problems that will arise and make me liquidate my business die, in the name of Jesus.

3. My source of wealth shall not decay in the name of Jesus.

4. O Lord, let every effort I put into business bring wealth in the name of Jesus.

PRAYER TO SILENCE FINANCIAL CRISES

5. I shall not work like an elephant and eat like ant in the name of Jesus.

6. Dark hunters assign against my business die in the name of Jesus.

7. Every leaking hole in my pocket, I seal you with blood of Jesus.

8. O Lord, give me wisdom that will make money work for me in the name of Jesus.

9. O Lord, bless me with farmer mentality in the name of Jesus.

10. Power to discover gold and build wealth fall upon me in the name of Jesus.

11. Power to build wealth, don't go elsewhere, my life is available, enter, in the name of Jesus.

12. O Lord, lead me through paths that will lead me to multiple streams of income in the name of Jesus.

13. My seed of success shall not die in the name of Jesus.

14. Every seed of hunter in my life wither and die in the name of Jesus.

15. Any dark hand that collects my money before it gets to me, wither in the name of Jesus.

16. Misplaced priority shall not be my portion in the name of Jesus.

17. I shall be a lender, not a borrower in the name of Jesus.

18. O Lord, expand my coast beyond human imagination in the name of Jesus.

19. Where others fail, I shall make it in the name of Jesus.

20. My head is located with ideas of fruitfulness in the name of Jesus.

21. Any power, assign to cut down tree of fruitfulness in my life die in the name of Jesus.

22. Thou agent of darkness assign to mislead me die in the name of Jesus.

23. Enemies of my success, I silence you, in the name of Jesus.

PRAYER TO SILENCE FINANCIAL CRISES

24. Every ambush against my business, scatter, in the name of Jesus.

25. I will not be helpless in business in the name of Jesus.

26. I am a king/queen, not a servant in the name of Jesus.

27. Every spirit of slavery assign against my life die in the name of Jesus.

28. Every enemy assign against my business, flee like birds to the mountain and perish in the name of Jesus.

29. Every curse pronounced against my business backfire in the name of Jesus.

30. Lord, repair the foundation of my business in the name of Jesus.

31. Every boast against my business, scatter to nothing in the name of Jesus.

32. Powers that refuse to let me go, die in the name of Jesus.

33. Dark association against my business, scatter in the name of Jesus.

34. Any power that wants to return me back to square one, die in the name of Jesus.

35. O Lord, trouble the power that trouble my business in the name of Jesus.

CHAPTER FIVE

RUN YOUR BUSINESS WELL

Running a business comes with a lot of challenges. Effective running is the core to expansion, profitability and wealth. A sound commercial in house base attracts customers. Business collapses if the capital injected is not well managed. Entrepreneur should put in creativity and drive for a business to grow. Hence, for a business to succeed there are ways you keep operations smooth and efficient.

First and foremost is to **lead by example**. Good harvest comes as a result of good leadership. The efforts you put in motivates employees to work hard for a good leadership. The efforts you put in motivates employee to work hard for a good return. As the boss, leading your team is not just about giving directives and laying down rules, it is about playing your role and keeping the goal in focus at all times. Employees take clue from their boss; and at times take clue from peers as well. Employees with loaded ideas have better opportunity to grow. Hence, their efforts measure for promotion in the nearest future.

As a leader, stay motivated and be on top of the game. Keep your eyes on your goal and be passionate about your business. In the face of challenges, don't quit but move on. It is when you are passionate about your business your heart will tell you, "Keep on; you will make it, use your skills to address the challenges".

Every business needs **right location**. The location of a business is very important to its survival and success. It is advisable to avoid rushing to take decision about where your business will be located. Many factors must be taken into consideration. The type of business you intend to do matters a lot. For instance, if you want to establish poultry, a shopping mall is not ideal, but an environment quiet and far from residential. Retail shops will take into consideration, shopping malls to hotels, airports, filling stations or residential areas. A mobile business must ensure that the vehicle used for the business is in good shape and suited for the business. Hence, you must know your target customer and keep the business close to them.

Safety is another point when you want to locate your business. In this time of terrorism and high crime rate, your business could become a target for robbers, vandals or destruction.

Business gold can only improve when you **take your customers seriously.** As business grow, don't take your customers for granted. The way you treat your customer on their first visit, is part of the reason they come back again. This is to say, customers service is a priority to keep them coming. Mind you, without the customers you will be out of business. Your wealth increases as more customers know and patronize you.

Many businesses that are battling for customers today once had customers queuing for their products and services. The fact is, they give qualitative service first, but failed to do so after some years in business. It is therefore necessary as an entrepreneur to do research and find out what is actually happening so as to retain customers and expand. You must set standard, improve and keep to it. Don't forget, there are competitors around you who are likely to not only copy you, but try to improve on it and have upper hand in the market. The idea is to start off strong, improve your standard and keep your staff motivated and happy. It is at this point; you can build wealth.

In career building or entrepreneurship it is advisable you **discover your 'golden time'** and concentrate on it. It is said, "If success is your goal, know your 'golden time'. What do we mean by 'golden time'? Your 'golden time' is the time you have the most focus and mental clarity of what to do. It is the time you are most effective in productivity.

At this period, time is friendly and favourable making tasks achieved with ease. It is thus advisable to mould your schedule around your 'golden time' to get the best of you. I pray, your golden time shall be discovered and not wasted. Amen.

In this era of information and climatic change, you must live up to expectation. You must therefore **involve in research** and follow happenings in the industry. In every industry there are facts or data upon which decision making ought to be based. When you ignore such information, you may end up with a business that is out-dated in the market. The fact is, competitors and consumers' expectations constantly change. To address this, you must constantly find out what people want, what is the trend and who are current competitors etc. Regardless of whether you have employees who are responsible to monitor such information, you need to have idea about it, so that you are not left in the cloud.

Many head are sold to the wind. When you lay hands on things and result keep failing, it is a problem. When you struggle without setting good result, there is a problem. When you dream and your head is attacked there is a problem. When you always find yourself in the midst of negatives, there is a problem. Your head may have been tampered with by dark powers. Hence, you need prayers to counter it. My book titled **MY HEAD IS NOT FOR SALE** shall address this.

Another important area of reflection to run a business well is the area of **insurance.** Every entrepreneur who sees his business as a source of livelihood will do everything possible to make it successful. The fact remains, majority of business men do not remember to insure their businesses when setting them up. They wave aside unforeseen circumstances capable of running them out of business. What they should do is to insure their business, which serves as the last straw when it comes to guiding against unforeseen contingencies in business. Insurance is the best mechanism to protect any business from unforeseen risks because it is the only institution that exists in order to ensure the continuity of other institutions because it restores them to their former positions whenever a loss occurs.

As a person, business man or business woman, you must **avoid scandal** by all means. Scandals destroy reputation and goodwill. Business won't remain the same if the name you built several years of toiling get spoilt in a day. No matter how clean a man or a company is, when the word is out, you can't take it back, and it will take real work, time and resources to clean your name. Scandals may rob you of opportunities because people are afraid to deal with you as a result of what they heard. Be it true or not, do everything possible to avoid scandal no matter what it will cost you. Protect your name, since you don't know where the next opportunity is coming from.

One important area that boosts business is to **avoid hoarding knowledge**. As the boss, employees look up to you to provide direction and leadership.

They expect you to know better than them or possibly 'know everything'! As a result, you mustn't be tempted to hoard information or knowledge. You boost staff morale, reduce cost, save time and above all, bring understanding and knowledge needed to make business a success, when you feed them with right information. When you share information with employees, they truly feel like a part of the company and make more effort towards its growth.

As an entrepreneur **stay creative**, wake up every day by thinking of ways to improve your business. By doing this, you are unlikely to get left behind as you may almost seize every opportunity to add something new and creative to your business.
Hence, it is important you make research a constant thing and review the performance of your business regularly. From this, you can deduce if you are doing better than last month, and what is responsible for the change.

In business **set target**, say ten years' target. During this time record your strengths and weakness in the course of time and how to improve on them for better result. Failure to set target which is an improvement on your initial target will only leave room for your competitors to displace you out of market.

Some years back, **Richard Branson** the founder of the virgin group and companies such as Virgin Atlantic, Virgin America, Virgin Mobile and Virgin Active was asked, "Your Company has hundreds of different business in operation- how do you manage to keep them on track and achieve expected output"?
He said, "The short answer is that I rely on a terrific team of CEOs and top managers, and on the great people around the world who work for virgin. But building this group was a long process"
One major point of all his response was, he made it through expansion. At the time he started student magazine and virgin records with his friends, he knew next to nothing about setting up a bureaucracy. As time went on they thought of expansion.

He said, "A few years later, as the number of our employees neared 100 at our record business, I began to fear we were becoming slow and cumbersome. So I split the company in half, which created a new company. We picked talented people from within virgin records to run it. The next time Virgin Records, number of employees reaches 100, I repeated this trick, and I have carried on doing it. This policy kept our business hungry and adaptable, and crucially, we uncovered great management talents – people who otherwise might not have gotten noticed, and would likely have pursued promotions at other companies. This kept our staff motivated".

One bold step is to **promote employees from within**. Really, when staff are promoted from within, there are, a plus from both strategic and financial point of view. Among them is, strong knowledge of the company, as employees understand company's organizational culture and operational protocols. They understand company's mission and are familiar with its task processes. When a staff is promoted from within, there is no delay or interruption in business continuity. The company also enjoy less overhead on recruiting process. Interview goes smoothly because the employee and employers are already familiar with one another and, there is likely less details or background information to check promoting from within. This increase staff morale and, thereby reduce employee turnover.

I pray every opportunity to accelerate your business shall locate you by fire. Amen.

PRAYER POINTS

1. Any power assign to take over my business in the spirit die in the name of Jesus.

2. Any profit I realize in my business shall not be swallowed by sickness in the name of Jesus.

3. Every wrong hand in my business, wither in the name of Jesus.

4. Helpers assign to push my business forward appear in the name of Jesus

5. O Lord, give me wisdom to lead by example in the name of Jesus

6. O Lord, direct my steps to right location, right place and people that will boost my business in the name of Jesus

7. Wisdom to win customers in business locate me by fire in the name of Jesus

PRAYER TO SILENCE FINANCIAL CRISES

8. My golden time, favour me in the name of Jesus.

9. I shall not waste opportunities God gives me in the name of Jesus.

10. Every satanic research and investigation to liquidate my business, scatter in the name of Jesus

11. Every scandal assign to silence me scatter in the name of Jesus

12. Business misfortune quit the corridor of my life in the name of Jesus

13. Lord Jesus, show your wonderful love in my business in the name of Jesus

14. Every arrow of liquidation fired against my business, backfire, in the name of Jesus

15. O Lord, provide me with faithful hands to run my business in the name of Jesus

16. I operate my business under the strong tower of God in the name of Jesus

17. Enemies shall not rejoice over me in the name of Jesus

18. Divine plan of God for my business manifest in the name of Jesus

19. Even at old age, my business shall outlive me in the name of Jesus.

20. My father and my God, give your angels charge over my business in the name of Jesus

21. Every adversaries against my business be disgraced in the name of Jesus

22. I envelope my business in the blood of Jesus

23. Blood of Jesus, fertilize my business and let it blossom in the name of Jesus

24. Light of heaven shine upon my business in the name of Jesus

25. I shall triumph over my enemies in the name of Jesus

26. I convert every curse upon my business to blessings in the name of Jesus

27. My business experience fruitfulness in the name of Jesus

28. Beauty and glory of God, overshadow my business in the name of Jesus

PRAYER TO SILENCE FINANCIAL CRISES

29. Working power miracles of God take control of my business in the name of Jesus

30. Every contrary diverse of tongues against my business scatter in the name of Jesus

31. Every contrary dedication of marine power against my business scatter in the name of Jesus

32. Every contrary dedication of witchcraft power against my business scatter in the name of Jesus

33. Every contrary dedication of idolatry against my business, scatter in the name of Jesus

34. Every arrow from home to liquidate my business, go back to your sender and consume them in the name of Jesus

35. Any witchcraft deposit in my business premises, die in the name of Jesus

36. By fire, by force, my business shall move forward in the name of Jesus

37. My business, arise and shine in the name of Jesus.

CHAPTER SIX

AVOID FINANCIAL CRISIS

Sadly, enough our economy is in shamble. We stagnate under visionless and selfish leaders where corruption is institutionalized. Here we are, our manufacturing companies are closing down as a result of hash economic policies, where power sector is neglected, couple with infrastructural decay, leading to worst brain drain since the day of slave trade era. The future is bleak making matters worse.

Brain drain is a signal of calamity to a nation, where gold (brain) of a nation is transferred (drain) elsewhere. This happens at the peak of economic crisis of a nation, when citizens run rat race for green pasture to other countries.

The observed reasons may be in the social environment of the source of a country in the form of lack of opportunities to develop revealed talents optimally, political instability, economic depression, health risks, security hazards, high power corruption, and collapse in educational system. The term brain drain was actually first coined by the Royal Society to describe the emigration of "Scientists and Technologists" to North America from Post-War European. Another source shows that the term was first used in the U.K to describe the influx of Indian Scientists and Engineers. In such situation, what a country is expected to enjoy is transferred elsewhere.

God deposited gold in the life everyone. To some it is gold in research, to some medicine, to some songs, to some academics, to some business, while some are good at production.

Pray, work hard and develop the intellectual property deposited in you. Whatever you do have focus and bring something out of it instead of speaking big fancy vocabulary. There are times we are so close to gold, even romance with it, eat it, but never knew it is gold. At times, we cut in pieces, destroy and dump our gold in the dustbin. Why? Because we lack knowledge and wisdom to make gold in us shine, rather we allow it perishes!

A CASE STUDY

We must strive hard and discover the gold in us. There is this Nigerian don that became first

African fellow of Academy of inventors. He is a Nigerian professor of Biology at Jackson State University, US, Ernest Izevbigie, who did research on bitter leaf, got patented as a food supplement for the prevention of cancer. Bitter leaf with botanical name vernonia amygdaline is a common plant in Africa yet no one knows it has medicinal value that can be developed to food supplement.

Gold doesn't form in life overnight; it is a matter of stages; so is patent right. In the case of Ernest, he extracted, purified, modified and tested the herb before he arrived at something. He said, "During the research, we have some breast cancer cells, which we exposed to extracts of this vernonia amygdaline, and we observed that it inhibited the growth of the cells. That was the first test. This observation was made around year 2000 and around 2001. We sought professional patent and it was granted in 2003. It was noted that we were the first to make that observation, patent are not given to an idea that already exist".

A patent lasts for 18 years before it expires. Brethren, why not do something and stop talks and complaints that takes you nowhere. I believe there is at least something in you that can put your name and your country in the world map.

The fact is, Ernest is taking a bold step further. He wants to develop this patent from nutricentical to pharmaceutical. Nutriceautical means something you can get that also has medicinal benefits, a food supplement. So to say, he wants to develop it into drug, so that it can be used as preventive and curable drug for cancer! This is Ernest, the Edo born, and American scholar for you. With the patent right granted, he shall overcome financial crisis. He discovered the gold in him.

Considering the low level of financial literacy among millions of people and global economic downtrend, many were caught in financial crisis. The fact is, financial crisis can affect anyone anytime. To claim you are financially responsible may not be enough to protect you from financial crisis, especially during economic recession.

This is the reason when caught in financial crisis rather than lament, "I am finished", build faith and believe you will overcome the obstacle before you; just as many others have done through the years.

No matter the challenge, if you approach the situation rightly, not only will you get through it, you will learn a lot which in turn will get you better prepare for the future.

At this point you may ask, what steps must I take when faced with financial crisis? The fact remains, there are several steps to take. In this chapter, we shall treat major steps that can make us fly high and silence threats of financial crisis that may roar at us like a deadly lion meeting us face to face. It is good you know and apply them for a better turnaround.

The first thing to do when faced with financial crisis is to **be calm and calculative.** Financial crisis comes as a surprise even when you see them coming. Therefore, build thick skin towards it and never panic, because it has come, and has come, solution is what you need, and must be provided. Remain calm as possible; otherwise the situation may be made worse. Panic comes with poor decision making. Panic makes you unsteady and if you take any step at this particular time, it may be a wrong step that leads to ruin. Imagine the reaction of Edison when his factory went into flames.

He never panicked. He built his company on that same spot, defeating spirit of fear and panic that would have stagnated him. He discovered gold in his reaction and build wealth that surpass human imagination.

The second step you may take is to **appraise your assets and liabilities to know your financial status,** your strengths and weaknesses, and opportunities and threats. There is need to appraise all existing assets and liabilities so as to determine the impact of financial crisis in your portfolio and to put things in proper perspective. It is only when you take stock of your assets can a true financial status be established and necessary action taken on how to rectify them.

The third step to take, when you want to walk out of financial crisis and build enduring wealth is to **spend wisely and think independence**, applying financial discipline and keep your spending within or below your income. It is a sacrifice to make that is why it is called delayed gratification. Some desires must be delayed today so that a better tomorrow can be achieved. Prioritize your financial obligations and responsibilities by understanding the need that are important and urgent, and ones that are neither important nor urgent.

Learn how to **prophesy good things into your head**. Catapult yourself with heavenly pole volt and occupy your economic position. It is at this point you look around and laugh. There and then, you will say, "I discover gold and build wealth". Yes, it is better said than done. Yet, you need to prophesy this into your life by using my book titled **830 PROPHECIES FOR THE HEAD.**

Know the difference between good debt and bad debt. Debt is a stranger we must avoid, mostly if it is one that will erode our financial status now and in the future. Good debt makes you richer while bad debt makes you poorer. To know where you belong on a debt scale it is good you take audit of your financial independence.

With good debt what you incur is repaid by others. It means, the item pays for itself. For example, if you borrow money to buy a car for car hire or haulage and the car pays for it and returns a profit, then you have a good debt. When you invest in property purchases such as homes, it is good debt because it appreciates in value, while rent accrued forms income. Student loan is said to be good debt invested in the future. What you receive as wages after graduation pays off the debt you incurred. They are investment in gold because in the process of incurring the debt you build wealth all along.

Your gold and wealth are in your assets. With assets, we refer to items that put money in your pocket, the money leaves and a part comes back. By the time the item is due for retirement; it has paid for itself many times over and still has some residual value which you can also redeem. Thus, you know where your money goes, and realize it many times over. This is wealth creation.

Bad debt on the other hand is a bad alternative. It is a debt you incur but repaid by yourself. The item you spent the money doesn't repay the loan. Very often, there would be nothing to show down the line. Borrowing money to acquire liabilities is misappropriation of funds. For example, renting property for long period is a bad debt. New vehicle purchased for leisure is a bad debt. High priced household purchase is a bad debt. These classes of debts are bad debts. They reduce family cash flow, wipe savings, put one under pressure, prevent family from achieving financial independence, lead to quarrel in the home and may put asunder what God joined together.

Fundamental to wealth creation is to **distinguish between purchases that end up in the thrash and those that are useful for a period of time**. Items that end up in the thrash are either useful for a short while and are discarded without value or are not used at all. Such items are classified as liabilities. You must know the content of your purchase, whether you are spending your income in assets or in liabilities.

You may be wondering what happen to your hard earned money each time you have a think back. You are amazed that such amount passed through your hands unaccounted for. You become sober and weak because you spend your money on liabilities.

With liabilities, your money goes and nothing comes back as residual, except few if any, that often have lower residual value. The mysteries of liabilities are they ended up in the thrash and refuse heap.

PRAYER TO SILENCE FINANCIAL CRISES

In such critical point, you ask yourself a number of financial questions like:

What percentage of my income goes into items that will end up in thrash?

What percentage of my income comes back after it has left my hand?
When the asset is due for sale can it retain some residual value?

When the asset is due for sale can it appreciate in value in the like of gold, precious stone, diamond or real estate?

When you are able to answer the questions above with affirmative you can then deduce if your purchase worth gold or it is a common financial nuisance at the end of the day.

Your cash flow is important and critical, and one way to know where the pendulum swings is to apply what is called **wealth conversion ratio**. Your wealth conversion ratio enables you to know the percentage of your income that comes back to you in a month, year, or in later years ahead. What it means is, you will be able to know if what you invest can be converted to money if you are cash strapped. This is important because the moment you run out of cash, you may start selling your property, at a giveaway price because you are desperate. To avoid this, you should put your money on items that has a good chance of appreciating over time, which means your money will eventually come back.

This wise way of detecting your cash flow saves you from burning a lot of cash without making progress financially because you avoid your purchase to end up in the thrash. Wealth conversion ratio enables you practice long term thinking with focus, by accumulating assets rather than liabilities. You are rich in gold when you buy what retains value, appreciate in value, will generate net positive returns in later years. By doing this, you don't give wings to your money to fly away, but hold it to create the future of your dreams.

In time of demand, it is essential you **differentiate between your needs and wants.** Many people end up spending their fortunes on things they do not need. They spend on what they want rather than what they need. For example, you need a car, but not one that will be expensive to maintain, or one that will advertise you for persecution. When you make costly mistake your money flies to waste dump.

Another important area that create wealth and give one a rest of mind is to **spend less than you earn**; keep your finance in order and avoid getting into debt or run out of cash before next pay day. If you don't spend all that you earn each month it means you will have some cash to save. Though, the fact remains, as a result of economic meltdown just picking up, corruption and waste that affects money in circulation, many barely have enough to feed.

Your wealth improves when you **spend some of it to develop yourself**. To do this, spend money to improve your knowledge, to acquire self-management and communication, or networking skills, which will not only help you to grow but enable you to manage yourself, your health and finances better.

To discover gold and build wealth **do not cultivate attitude to impress others** that may eventually affect you. You are likely to cause financial problems for yourself when you buy or do things to impress others. Doing this, makes you live above your means. It is also likely you invest on items you don't need.

Some years ago a boy sold his kidney through the internet to get iPhone. The iPhone will look good and acceptable to ordinary eyes but with future repercussion. The fact is, as the iPhone reduces in value or is out of fashion, his life diminishes as well. He signed his death warrant and dug his grave the day he sealed the contract.

To handle money well and build wealth, **avoid too much entertainment**. It is not every burial ceremony you must attend. It is not all clothes presented to you as family cloth (Aso Ebi) you must subscribe to. When you limit attending 'dead' ceremonies, your financial responsibility will be low. Hence, panic, shame and financial waste will reduce.

The amount of money people spend on entertainment and food has resulted in phrases,

"Eating your future", "Eating the seeds that yield tomorrow". To some people every little thing demands celebration. For example, when they buy fairly used television set, they celebrate it, using the term, "We are washing it", when they buy fairly used carpet or rug, they "wash it". With such people, it is celebration galore when they purchase fairly used car, called *tokunbo* car in Nigeria. It doesn't end there, when they are promoted in office, when they mark birthdays, when they receive awards, when they do naming ceremony or granted visa to overseas country, they involve themselves in 'crazy' entertainments.

To them everything virtually calls for celebration. Instead of keeping their expenses in check and secure their future, they waste it away. Brethren, if you fall into this group, I endure you to consider your earnings and plan for the future. Be smart enough to avoid what can be avoided so that you can discover gold with your earnings.

Another way forward in wealth creation is to **access information** to know what operates in the market, to know new, and or, changing policies, and to know investment situation. Available information may be discussed with people of professional ethics to have better understanding of present situation and steps to take.

You can discover gold in your **action plan**. This can be done by creating action plan that will guide you in every step you take. You may seek assistance of financial experts who can draw holistic strategy that gives your plan a fine economic face.

In the new plan, you are expected to marry yourself to what may boost you economically and do away with luxuries that breed waste. Such steps may include, doing away with eating out, cinema visits, shopping frees and questionable entertainments. Savings realized can serve as buffer for your portfolio.

If you are entangle in loan repayment, a loan repayment plan can be included in the action plan in a bid to gradually free you from debt or revise the terms thereof.

In running your business, aspire to **support your vocational skills with entrepreneurial skills.** Your vocational skill talks about technical knowhow of the business while entrepreneurial skill is about how to run the business.

The two are inseparable as both enable you to do your business with passion and vision for life. Alas, it enables you go further to acquire necessary business skills to transform your vision into reality. That way, if there are challenges along the way, your heart will tell you, "Keep on you will make it" and then you will start using your skills to address the challenge.

As an entrepreneur, you must **be knowledgeable of your business**, or else, you will be working for others, even in matters as simple as buying and selling. In Nigeria today, you open a shop, you equip it, you bring somebody there to come and work for you and before you know it, he understands what is selling fast and starts to buy his supplies. When you come back to take stock, he would tell you, "I have sold one piece of this item"; whereas he has sold ten pieces. He sold nine pieces for himself.

In business and daily activities, **budget** plays vital role. Apart from financial freedom that expose you to wealth creation; budgeting is one of the most important aspects of money management. If you don't manage your money well, it shall disappear before you know it. You overcome financial crisis when you control your expenses, stick to viable projects and adjust when necessary.

Budgets help you to effectively execute your financial plan. With budget you become a financially responsible person, especially when you have spending problems. It helps avoid unnecessary purchase and enables you live within your means. It helps you to know your financial stand. By planning your expenses ahead and determining what to spend on every item you need, you will have more money at your disposal. By this, it will help prevent your debt from rising and reduce it. Budget will guide you to achieve your goal and vision. This is so, because budget helps you spend less, and you have more money available to pursue your goal.

If you feel so concerned and serious about your business idea and you don't have money then **look**

for a partner, pool your money together and start the business. Run it at the small scale that your money allows. When you build tract record and now looking for a third party, may be a bank, to give you money, they will see the seriousness with which you have run the business and you may be asking for one million naira and they will say, "Why not take two million naira". Why do they do this? It is because they discover gold in you.

You don't form partnership for the sake of it. But for benefits that accrue from it. Those who form partnership with such view shall witness failure. Going into business with others or friends must be a thing you think about seriously. Those who form partnership on wrong platform experience failure. Partnership is going into business with people you share the same values and work ethics to overcome funding and skill challenges.

This doesn't mean you must have same strength and weakness, because the idea is for you to complement each other. By this, your ideal partner should be strong in area where you are weak and vice versa. In business, have clear idea of what each partner brings to the table, contacts, funds, experience, creativity, ideas, or innovation. If you are starting a new business in which you have limited experience, there is nothing wrong in getting a partner who is more experience than you are. There is nothing wrong with one partner being the brain and the other the muscle. It is at such point the gold in both of you can be discovered and wealth created.

Anytime you go into partnership, it is necessary you have formal partnership agreement. Don't wait until business breakeven or when it grows into a big company. Before you enter into partnership, consider where misunderstanding and disagreement may arise in the future. To avoid this, consider the followings in your agreement

Know what the initial contribution of each partner will be

Know how disputes will be settled.

Know how profits and losses will be shared

Know what each partner will pay and or compensation will be

Know how the business will function if a partner becomes incapacitated.

Know the provisions for making changes to the partner, or to dissolving it.

Know how the assets of the partnership will be distributed if dissolved. When you know all these, it becomes simple and easy to paddle the canoe of the business, by putting efforts into it without fear. Your joint efforts shall bring out the best in you and enable you build wealth. In every business, when you foresee a gap in the market take it, and if a new business has the potential to damage your brand in any way, you should not invest in it.

As an entrepreneur you can decide to **invest in managed funds** handled by professionals on your behalf. The units of managed funds are collectively known as mutual funds. Professionals that will help you manage it; will advise the right time to invest and when to withdraw. Professionals will also advise you the right ones to invest in. You need them as brokers for a token fee to supply you with valuable investment information and suggestions to make profitable investment. This investment portfolio of mutual funds or stocks a firm manages is called **wrap accounts**. As client, you won't be left in the dark as regard the goings in the market; you would be frequently supplied with market reviews and analysis, and profitable investment suggestions.

Mutual funds are large and diversified portfolios of securities, selected by skilled security professionals and market analysts, and managed by highly qualify investment professional. Mutual funds have portfolio managers and a research team, whose duty it is to choose the best possible securities to add to the fund portfolio.

Also, a mutual fund makes it easy for investors to move in and out easily, as the funds can be sold at short notice with little difference between the sales price and the most current market value.

A way to make your gold robust and enlarge your economic coast is to **develop multiple streams of income** rather than develop on one income source when you know exactly what it is you want to do. A good place to start is having your money work for you- putting your savings to work. You don't just dump money in your account; rather make friends with your bank to know which portfolio available you can invest with your savings. They will gladly educate you on the range of products available in your banks. Your banker will often match that rate rather than allow you to walk away.

In whatever business you are into, service or production, as addition to your source of income, have it at the back of your mind that **you are doing it, for which you will be rewarded.** This means service and product shall come first, before you think of reward or profit. If you look for money – profit first; you may provide poor product or service, which may drive away customers.

Couples must address the way they spend and pay back. Taking a loan simply means accessing money you are yet to earn, and spending tomorrow's money today. It is not evil in accessing a loan, if the money shall create wealth to pay itself. But then, couples should build financial independence on the notion that love does not solve money problems. You must discuss and agree on how you intend to manage as couple.

A woman must not shift all the responsibilities in the home on her husband, while a man shouldn't shift the responsibility in the home on his wife as well. There should be an understanding when couple comes together. Many husbands have borrowed money to please their wives, buying gifts they cannot afford or going on holiday funded by credit card. Everything goes smoothly until the bills start to arrive. If you don't handle your finances properly, your love nest may turn to a matrimonial shouting festival and in some instances, boxing ring and domestic violence. It can be very frustrating when one partner is trying hard to build while the other is busy pulling it all down. In such a situation, it will be difficult to build atmosphere that generates wealth.

It is written, the love of money is the root of all evil, but the lack of money is the root of bitterness. Money may not buy love, but without money, love can suffocate. Couples should therefore create atmosphere to know the true financial state of things, and not where every partner is doing his or her thing while the pile of debt keeps going up, creating more tension in the home. In such situation, how can you dig gold? If we don't exercise proper control over our finance, it can cost us our home, business, value, friendship, marriage, sanity and life. That is why it makes no sense to mortgage our future in order to please people in the present.

There is field of gold in your home only if you can discover it. Couples should come together as one, live as one, do things as one and love each other as one. Only then can they discover gold and build wealth.

Another area that causes financial crisis is **lending money to friends**, who often not pay back. Money and friendship often doesn't mix very well. Money can part the best of friends or cause sour relationship. It is easy to present reasons why the money is needed, but when it is time to pay, the song is different. He starts offering excuses even in instances when none is demanded. Soon, he begins to avoid his once lovely friend. It is at this point; the borrower expects the lender should be more understanding. The borrower feels the lender should write off the debt entirely, especially when the lender seems relatively much better off financially than the borrower.

Friends use blackmail and at times manipulation to get what they want. They demand when they suspect that their friend(s) have received salary, or suspect there is a surplus in terms of a bonus, pay rise, an unexpected wind fall etc. Most times, they borrow with no intent to pay back.

To avoid financial misunderstanding learn to say no, so that you are not labeled People's Bank. Rather than be a People's Bank, put your excess or savings in the money market to work for you.

To do this, it means your money is not available to start with. Another very good protection measure is to lend your friend little money knowing full well he will not pay back. He won't ask for more when he hasn't pay the previous one he borrowed. Though there are times, a friend may be stubborn by coming for more, while what he borrowed last wasn't paid. It is not an offense, he only came, and you as well is not mandatory to lend. To keep friendship going, what may be good answer is, "I could have given you, but I need a little cash urgently now, and if you can pay me what I lend you last time, I will be glad, so that I don't miss the upcoming opportunity. My money is hanging over there, and as a friend I know you won't let me down. When can I have the money back?" The answer will put him off.

To discourage friends to 'naked' you financially through borrowing I suggest you apply 5% approach method. By this, if a friend comes for money, calculate 5% of what he requested and give him. Make sure you don't reveal your method to friends, not even your spouse because if it is eventually known as your method, they may come for a large amount of money knowing well that when you calculate 5% of the money, it will be exactly what they need. For example, someone that needs N25,000 may come and ask for N500,000 knowing full well you will calculate 5% of N500,000 which will arrive at what he needs. I advise you should be careful and intelligent of how you handle issues.

I pray, the wisdom God gave you shall not perish in the name of Jesus. Amen.

PRAYER POINTS

1. Covenant of failure upon my business break in the name of Jesus

2. The gold God deposited in me shall not die in the name of Jesus

3. The gold in my business shall not expire in the name of Jesus

4. Any power drawing me back as I move close to success die in the name of Jesus

5. Every battle assign to swallow my wealth scatter in the name of Jesus

6. Every obstacle standing between me and success die in the name of Jesus

7. No matter the challenge against my business I shall succeed in the name of Jesus

8. Lord, give me power and ability to live above any form of financial crisis that may arise against my business in the name of Jesus

9. Business liabilities shall not swallow my asset in the name of Jesus

10. I shall not go about with portfolio of failure in the name of Jesus

11. I convert every financial crisis to financial abundance in the name of Jesus

12. Lord, load me with wisdom of financial independence in the name of Jesus

PRAYER TO SILENCE FINANCIAL CRISES

13. I lay hands on good business that accelerate wealth in the name of Jesus

14. I shall not borrow before I feed in the name of Jesus

15. I seal every manner of leaking pocket troubling my finance in the name of Jesus

16. Lord, let people that will feed me with information to grow locate me in the name of Jesus

17. Lord, bless me with skill to take my business to the next level in the name of Jesus

18. Any power or personality, assign to sink my business, experience double failure and disgrace in the name of Jesus

19. Spirit of rejection assign against my business die in the name of Jesus

20. Spirit of stagnation assign against my business; be nullified in the name of Jesus

21. Spirit of failure assign against my business die in the name of Jesus

22. Negative judgment in the spirit against my business; be nullified in the name of Jesus

23. Spirit of mismanagement assign against my business die in the name of Jesus

24. Lord Jesus, use your blood to redeem my business in the name of Jesus.

25. Every magical power fashioned against my business die in the name of Jesus

26. Spirit of robbery, assign to attack my business, die, in the name of Jesus

27. Mercy and favour of God, take over my business in the name of Jesus

28. I shall record profit not losses in business in the name of Jesus

29. Every decay spirit associated with my business, carry your load and die in the name of Jesus.

30. I speak woe against authority and dominion of Satan upon my life in the name of Jesus.

31. I claim surplus miracles in my business in the name of Jesus

PRAYER TO SILENCE FINANCIAL CRISES

32. I pull down every stronghold of Satan against my business in the name of Jesus

33. Every chain of failure assign to pull my business down, break to pieces in the name of Jesus

34. Every embargo against my business break in the name of Jesus

35. Yoke of failure upon my business break in the name of Jesus

36. I pour divine salt to the source of my business to heal and improve it in the name of Jesus.

37. Spirit of wasters in my business die in the name of Jesus

37. Every cloud of bewitchment upon my business clear away in the name of Jesus

39. I prophesy success into my business in the name of Jesus.

CHAPTER SEVEN

DISCOVER GOLD IN STOCKS

Stock market is another avenue to make wealth if you are versed in its operations. The focal point whenever you want to invest in it is to know which company you will invest, how to invest and when to invest in the stock market. Stock market is what you don't do in isolation. Investing in stock require a little bit of investigation intelligence, and due diligence. The fact is, investing in shares is the same as investing in the company that issued the shares. As an investor, you should be interested in the shares as well as in the company that owns the share.

Like a coin that has two sides, stock market has its bad and good sides. While many smile to banks as a result of dividends allotment, or sale of shares, some have their fingers burnt in the process.

A wise investor would win most of the time and build wealth. This is possible if certain conditions are followed. We shall discuss these one after another.
The first thing to do as an investor is to study and analyze the company you wish to invest. If you don't have a time or tools to carry out the analysis,

you should employ the services of an expert. But then, it is advisable you know at least something about the company, if not everything before you invest.

In doing this, you must show interest in the people running the company. To achieve this, you may include the products or services of the company, composition of the board; interests of the directors; performance of the company, composition in the industry and future prospects, among others.

Information about a company is essential. In information gathering, you don't necessarily have to see the director of the company. You can get firsthand information from the receptions desk. Such information may give you next step to take. It is also good if you can familiarize yourself with annual reports of companies. This shall save you from a lot of investment mistakes. Though, caution should be sound here, as you must not be carried away by the results you see on the pages of newspapers, because most companies do publish absolute figures. They may declare fabulous profit in pages of newspapers without telling you they will pay some debts or pay bank loans that would wipe off all the profit.

This is the reason anybody who wants to make money in an enduring manner must know how to analyze annual reports and accounts, and it is not that difficult.

In this manner, what an investor should do is to check the prospectus to see if they meet expectation. Thus, an investor needs to check the integrity of the financial information a company provides and make himself a friend of annual reports and accounts of companies. A prospectus gives a lot of this information You can as well do elementary financial ratio by checking whether a company is doing well or not. An investor who wants to make money must acquire basic ability to analyze companies and not base everything on speculation.

A wise investor should have good investment plan and stock picking strategy. When picking stock, the analysis of company's past experience should serve as guide. Such past performance should be indicative of what the future holds for such a company.

There is the need to adopt long-term prospective if you want to be a wise investor, as capital markets is a market for long term funds. You may be disappointed if you come in thinking of making quick money on the short run.

Though, it is possible to make significant gain in a short period, it is better to have a long term view.
It is therefore necessary to clarify your objectives before you invest. Are you a speculator or you are in for long term business? A long term investor won't panic, unlike a speculator. Someone who invests in shares in First Bank PLC won't panic because he expects bonus and dividends along the line.

Learn when to exit, plan your exit time as well. Set your exit triggers and act on them. Hence, it is paramount to **know your entrance and exit time**. The wise investor should set an exit target once that target has been attained, it is advisable to sell and go for lower priced stocks that will grow in a short while. In other word, a wise investor will try not to be greedy when stock price continues to rise. At the point at which you want to go in, you must have determine the price you want the stock to rise to before you get out. This point is called **stock fair value point.**

Buying shares in capital market is not the only way to wealth creation. You can spread out a bit **buying bonds in the capital market**. To insulate you from market risks, it is advisable you go into bond market. A decision to buy stocks could result in loses, but with bonds you can go to sleep. The reason is you can be assured of fixed income from your investment.

This can be achieved through **investment in fixed and steady income securities**, also known as debt securities in the capital market. The return of a fixed income is known in advance. The bond market is a stable and safe investment option, especially in a **bearish market** (when prices of stocks are on the decline) thus, as an investor it makes sense to have at least part of your portfolio invested in bonds.

Fixed income securities abound in money and capital markets. In the money market are short-term instruments, like treasury bills, and the conventional fixed deposit accounts. They usually have tenors of less than a year, and so investors can actually earn fixed incomes, which for treasury bills, is given in form of a discount or interests, and fixed deposit accounts, also interests.

Another vital area of gold mine creation is **mutual bond investment**. Wise investors must diversify their investments across all the sectors of the market. Mutual bond serves this purpose. A mutual bond is a company that brings together money from many people and invests it in stocks, bonds or other securities. It is also called **"guaranteed funds"**. It is a portfolio that guarantees capital invested will not be eroded, even in part.

Mutual funds are good vehicles for people to invest in stocks because they are managed by professionals. They also enable investor own shares in many companies instead of buying individual stocks or bonds directly. This helps to spread risk.

The advantage of mutual fund investment is that an investor does not need to worry that his money can disappear, though returns can still be relatively lower than if trading directly on the market. From research, some give an assurance that funds invested will yield a minimum return of 13 percent annually. It may be small, but here you don't leave your money dormant in the bank, and or, where your account is debited for one reason or the other under different strange names!

As an investor, you can also **invest in real estate**, though it is not capital market investment. Real estate investment pay off as it appreciates over time. This is perhaps the most solid investment anyone can make. It appreciates in value and income from rent, and can be assumed to grow in a consistent manner over time.

Real estate is generally well protected as long as the titles are perfected and the property is not located in an area that government can acquire "for public use" or prone to environmental disaster, such as flooding.

A CASE STUDY

There was this case of a man who built one of his houses in eye brow area many years back. This building was his first house. He built the house for about N12, 000:00 with a loan. After a while, he had some money and went to the outskirt of the city, a typical bush and bought a plot of land. He couldn't develop it because he was cash trapped.

Three years later he developed the land and built a bungalow. As time went by he bought another two plots of land and fenced it.

His first building doesn't yield income much because it is a residential home. Tenants owed rents. One day, a bank approached him to buy it and a deal was struck. He eventually sold it for 30 million naira! This is real estate for you.

The last bond or investment, I will advise you to make is **health insurance scheme or bond.** The reason I mention it last is, everyone plans for old age. No one pray for untimely death.

I pray that untimely death shall not be your portion. Amen. To go for health care insurance means you are tidying up to protect your loved one from serious headaches after you are gone. Also, old age could come with some health problems, so investing in a healthcare plan with any of the certified healthcare companies is advisable.

The most important thing at this point is for one to **put his house in order**. Jacob did this when he blessed his children. The blessing can be likened to stock in the spirit that yielded in years to come. In the case of stocks, assets should be well documented in a Will. A Will allows for an orderly transfer of assets after you are gone. Get a lawyer to do this. To write a Will means you don't want your asset to scatter into the wind.

It is also possible to **set up a trust** and transfer your assets to your intended beneficiaries that are still young.

Also, if a man wants his wife or children to inherit his property, he can simply **make a deed of gift and bequeath the asset to the intended beneficiary.** In case the beneficiary is a minor, the benefactor could make himself a trustee of the assets for the child or minor.

On a final note, reorganize your portfolio to date. You can do this by creating a file that lists all your account numbers, phone numbers of stockbrokers and bankers, and important documents such as your Will. Keep it in a safe and easily accessible place for trusted family members in case something happens to you.

Central Securities Clearing System (C.S.C.S.) AND YOU

There is the old belief of keeping share certificates in a cupboard at home or have them framed and hanged on the wall, feeling a comforting sense of wealth as they are admired. This is an old fashion of documentation. The Nigerian Stock Exchange has been steadily phasing out issuance of share certificates as Nigerian capital markets are urged to comply with its directive to "dematerialize" share certificates.

What this boils down to is that share certificates will soon go out of existence, as shareholders are expected to transfer their existing share certificates to an electronic share settlement system, which will ultimately render paper certificates obsolete.

To achieve this, the Nigerian capital market established the Central Securities Clearing System (C.S.C.S.), which commenced operation in 1997.

What are the importance of keeping your shares in the C.S.C.S. depository? Can there be gold in it? Can wealth be created as a result? The answer is capital YES. When we study the underlying importance, you will have no option than to visit your stockbroker and have your certificates dematerialized. When an investor opens a C.S.C.S. account, the shareholder's data is captured or transferred into an electronic register and an equivalent number of securities are credited in electronic form to the C.S.C.S. depository.

The paper share certificates are replaced by electronic systems to reflect shareholders current value. When your certificates are dematerialized, it facilitates paperless trading whereby transactions are executed electronically. As a result, an up-to-date record is kept as new transactions are effected as at when transacted.

Your investment is safeguarded when you lodge your shares in a C.S.C.S. account. This is so because it eliminates the risk of loss of documents, of theft, fraudulent transactions, or extreme risks, such as fire or flooding, which are hazards investors may face when they keep their share certificates at home. Thus, the burden of storage and handling of your share certificates is taken off you.

With C.S.C.S. account in place, fraud is kept at low base as a trade alert system is in place, which will alert you by text should any transaction be made on your account.

When certificates are dematerialized, it ends the challenge of annual printing, sorting and dispatching of certificates to shareholders from the registrar's office. The anxieties shareholders pass through when they don't receive their share certificates end with the introduction of C.S.C.S. account.

When you buy new shares through a public offer or by a right issue, it becomes easier for your account to be updated.

All you need is to quote your C.S.C.S. account number, the number of shares you applied for on the form, and the number allotted to you, which will be credited directly to your C.S.C.S. account. Thus, attendant lost in transit or delay in receiving your certificate is avoided.

To operate a C.S.C.S. account ease sales of shares. If you hold paper certificates and wish to trade your shares, you could be subjected to delays in verification process, which can sometimes be long and tedious. The effect of this is that in time of price variation, when shares move against you, you will not be able to sell your shares until your share certificate is dematerialized. You may lose out instead of making gains. But, for someone with a C.S.C.S. account, it will be easy for the registrar to verify account and signature quickly. It will enable him to take advantage of market situation, particularly in a volatile time.

A C.S.C.S. account boosts your borrowing power. Mostly when you wish to borrow using your shares as collateral, your banker or other lender will want the certificates lodged and verified into a C.S.C.S. account. Without this in place, your transaction could be delayed.

The C.S.C.S. is operated online at website www.cscsnigerialtd.com. By this, registered investors can monitor their investments at anytime and from anywhere in the world. Here, you can view your C.S.C.S. stock account statements, obtain your stock position regularly, review and evaluate your portfolios. You can as well monitor stock prices and new stock deposits into the C.S.C.S.

Above all, C.S.C.S. stock accounts increase the efficiency and liquidity of the market, raise investor confidence, leading to a more vibrant and transparent capital market. Hence, as a shareholder, you experience gold in shares that build wealth.

I pray, your efforts and labour shall not end in vain. Amen.

PRAYER TO SILENCE FINANCIAL CRISES

PRAYER POINTS

1. O Lord, direct my step to where I shall make fortunes in the name of Jesus.

2. My wealth shall not disappear to the wind in the name of Jesus

3. Wisdom to build wealth occupy my mind in the name of Jesus

4. I shall not meet wrong people that will scatter my finance in the name of Jesus.

5. Any satanic animal that swallow my fortunes, vomit them now in the name of Jesus

6. I shall be a lender not a borrower in the name of Jesus

7. I shall occupy the head and not the tail region in the name of Jesus

8. Every cloud assign against my business clear away in the name of Jesus

9. Parasites in my business die in the name of Jesus

10. Every stronghold of poverty fashioned against my destiny, I dismantle you in the name of Jesus.

11. Serpents and scorpions against my destiny die in the name of Jesus.

12. Covenant of failure against my career break in the name of Jesus

13. Satanic representatives assign to pull me down, die in your mission in the name of Jesus

14. Every foundational bondage affecting my destiny, break in the name of Jesus

15. Witchcraft magnet assign to scatter my business break to pieces in the name of Jesus

16. Plantation of misfortune in my business die to your root in the name of Jesus.

17. Every sacrifice done in order to harm me backfire in the name of Jesus

18. Evil farmer planting weeds in my investment to tormented me die in the name of Jesus

19. I refuse to lay hands on unprofitable ventures in the name of Jesus

20. My helpers in captivity receive freedom and locate me in the name of Jesus.

PRAYER TO SILENCE FINANCIAL CRISES

21. My finances trapped in the darkroom of Satan, be released unto me in the name of Jesus

22. Spirit of failure and defeat shall not take over my life in the name of Jesus

23. I receive anointing of excellence in the name of Jesus

24. Business swallower, vomit my business and die in the name of Jesus

25. I revoke satanic ownership on my investment in the name of Jesus

26. I shall not be robbed of the right to my investment in the name of Jesus

27. Every weapon formed against my investment shall not prosper in the name of Jesus

28. My destiny, reject poverty in the name of Jesus

29. Thou eagle of my destiny fly high, occupy your position in the name of Jesus

30. Yoke of poverty upon my life break in the name of Jesus

31. Dark agenda against my business scatter in the name of Jesus

32. Arrow of financial failure fired against me backfire in the name of Jesus

33. Every witchcraft chain assign to pull down my business break to pieces in the name of Jesus

34. I declare myself, Mr. Bundle of Breakthroughs and Happiness in the name of Jesus

CHAPTER EIGHT
GOLD AND WEALTH IN DIET

All wealth made, all wealth acquired or accumulated without good health is a waste. There is gold, wealth, happiness and joy in the food we eat. As you age, feed on good foods that strengthen the soul and body. At the same time, watch what you eat, don't eat anyhow, but qualitative food.

There is joy in the food you eat that makes you healthy and young. To maintain a healthy and well-balanced diet is one approach. The good news is that there are some foods that are thought to give extra ammunition when it comes to combating the signs of ageing. By eating right food and paying attention to diet, you can drastically improve your appearance.

I shall dedicate this chapter wholly to plant-based diet- fruit. Really, we follow a plant-based diet for different reasons religious, cultural, or ethical and to stay away from health problems. The book of Ezekiel 47:12 says, *"...Their fruit will serve for food and their leaves for healing"* Thus, to eat plant based food is not only hygienic but biblical.

Fruit is the most important food we can possibly eat. All the vitamins, minerals, carbohydrates, amino acids as well as fatty acids the human body requires for existence are found in fruits.

There is a dietary law pertaining to fruit consumption. It may look amazing to say that, fruit should never be eaten with, or immediately following anything. In essence, fruit has to be eaten on an empty stomach. Oh yes, this is the proper way to eat fruit. Eat fruit first before you eat food!

The fact is, fruit eaten on top of other foods creates problems in digestive tract. The fruit is ready to go straight through the stomach into the intestines, but it is prevented from doing so by delicious meal. It is said that the very instant that fruit comes in contact with the food in the stomach and digestive juices, the entire meal rots and ferments and turns to acid, thereby, causing discomfort.

Another rule is, eat washed or clean fruit that is washed and uncooked. Avoid fruit that has been altered in any way by heat. It doesn't supply any nutrients; canned fruits, fruit pies, baked pineapple and apple are good examples.

We shall treat a number fruits and see how good they are to the body. This doesn't mean other foods are not good, but tells reasons we must keep our table with fruits.

CUCUMBER

Even in the face of manna, the children of Israel crave for cucumber. They said in protest, ***"We remember the fish we ate in Egypt at no cost- also the cucumbers, melons, leeks, onions and garlic. But now we have lost our appetite, we never see anything but this manna"!*** Numbers 11:5-6.

What is cucumber? It is a very edible and nutritious vegetable which comes from the cucumber plant, cucumis satives. It is a low calorie vegetable and has more to offer you than just water. It can be eaten raw; in vegetable salads; or drink in form of juice, or cooked. With so many health benefits, it becomes one of the important parts of a good diet. So, why should we eat cucumbers?

Cucumber is 90 percent water and is very rich in vitamin. It is known to be cooling agent due to the water in it.

Being a low calorie vegetable, it provides just 15 calories per 100g. It contains no saturated fats or cholesterol.

Cucumber peel is a good source of dietary fibre that helps reduce constipation, and offers some protection against colon cancers by eliminating toxic compounds from gut.

It is very good source of potassium, which is a heart-friendly electrolyte.

For those suffering from high blood pressure they should eat cucumber to counter the effects of sodium.

For weight loss, eat cucumber to put your weight in check through its high water and potassium content.

The water content in cucumber is more nutritious than regular water. It keeps you hydrated, thus regulating your body temperature. It also helps in flushing out the toxins from the body.

The high water content, vitamins A, B and C and the presence of certain minerals such as magnesium, potassium, and silicon make cucumber an essential part of skin care.

When used as eye pads, cucumber relieves puffiness and swelling around the eyes, as well as the dark circles under the eyes. This is because cucumber contains ascorbic and caffeic acid, both of which prevent water retention.

Cucumber juice is good for teeth and gums problems. Its dietary fiber is good for teeth and gums.

Cucumber seeds are used as a natural remedy for treating tapeworms. Bruised cucumber seeds mixed with water are also effective in the treatment of swellings of the mucous membranes of the nose and the throat.

Cucumber relieves gout and arthritis pain because it is rich in vitamins A, B1, B6, C and D, foliate, Calcium, Magnesium and Potassium.

Cucumber juice helps diabetic patients

What more? A glass of fresh cucumber juice sends digestive disordered-acidity, heartburn, gastritis and even ulcers-parking! There are wonders, wealth, gold, miracles, good health and joy in the train of cucumber!

WATERMELON

Watermelon is round; oblong or spherical in shape. It features thick green rinds that are often spotted or stripped. It has 90 percent water content. It has easy-to eat texture which makes it a favourite thirst-quenching fruit. Inside it is deep red-pink colour with seeds that are black, brown, white, green or yellow, and a few varieties are actually seedless.

One of the best ways of choosing a flavourful melon is to look at the colour. When choosing a whole watermelon get one that is heavy for its size with smooth body; or one which has an area that is distinct in colour from the rest, displaying a yellowish or creamy tone? This is the underbelly, the place that was resting on the ground during ripening, and if the fruit does not have this marking, it may have been harvested prematurely, which will negatively affect its taste, texture and juiciness. Eating the meat of the fruit is the best way to take advantage of all its nutrients.

So, what do you gain eating watermelon?
The fact is, both the flesh and seed of watermelon are nutritious. The flesh contain vitamin A, B and C, while the seeds contain selenium, essential fats, zinc and vitamin E, all of which help against free radical damage and aging.

Watermelon is a source of carotene antioxidant which is called lycopene. These antioxidants travel throughout the body neutralizing free radicals. Free radicals are substances in the body that can cause much damage. They are able to oxidize cholesterol, making it stick to blood vessel walls and thicken them which can lead to heart attack or stroke. So, lycopene which gives fruits the attractive red colour can help reduce the risks of prostate cancer.

Watermelon is rich in the B vitamins, which is good for energy production. Also, it is a very good source of vitamin B6, B1 and magnesium.

Watermelon has antioxidants that help reduce the severity of asthma. It also reduces the risk of colon cancer, heart disease and arthritis.

Watermelon is a good source of thiamin, potassium, and magnesium which protect the body from many diseases.
Watermelon is loaded with healing and good health. Why not go for it today and claim gold and wealth abound in it.

WONDERS OF WATERMELON SEEDS

There are wonders and benefits in consuming watermelon seeds. Watermelon seeds make a great snack when they have been dried and roasted. Their nutritional value is unlimited when they are eaten. Prepared seeds of watermelons include; protein, B vitamins and minerals.

PROTEIN: Watermelon seeds are very high in protein, which consists of several amino acids, one of which is argentine, with benefits of regulating blood pressure and treating of coronary heart disease.

B VITAMINS: Watermelon seeds are loaded with several of the B vitamins necessary for converting food into energy and other important body functions.

The most prevalent B vitamins in watermelon seeds is niacin, which is important for maintaining the nervous and digestive systems, and skin health.

MINERAL: Minerals abound in watermelon seeds, with magnesium as the most abundant. Magnesium helps regulate blood pressure.

BITTER LEAF JUICE

Bitter leaf juice is gold in itself. The botanical name for bitter leaf is Veronina Amygdaline. Among the Yorubas in Nigeria, it is known as Ewuro, it is called Shiwaka by the Hausas and called Olugbu among the Igbos in Nigeria.

Bitter leaf is readily found everywhere. It is a simple inexpensive natural herb you can use to ensure optimum health and wellbeing. The fact is we are so blessed with diverse array of potent herbs and plants with benefits and natural healing ability.

Funny enough, every day we do one of two things, build health or produce disease in ourselves. What you eat or drink kills you gradually or builds you. The name alone 'bitter leaf' makes it the least on the table giving our love for sugar, sodium and chemical laden options that are readily at our reach. Our delicacies are sugar-centric and therefore not fond of bitter tasting food.

But then, life is all about choices. We choose to take responsibility for our health and well-being. There are different herbs, plants, fruits and vegetables we juice and drink to detoxify, maintain optimum health or help cure certain ailments.

To enjoy bitter leaf better for optimum healing, it is good to juice it for a cool drink. Juicing it is far better than boiling it. To get its full potency and medicinal value, bitter leaf should be juiced raw.

Here are some of the health benefits of juicing your bitter leaf.

It is a liver herb that stimulates, cleanse and support the liver and gall bladder

It stimulates nervous system and immune system function

It combats fatigue and exhaustion

PRAYER TO SILENCE FINANCIAL CRISES

It improves digestion

It does internal cleansing

It helps with diabetes, by drastically reducing sugar level
It is a great remedy for stomach ache.

It stimulates the gut wall's self-repair mechanism

It increases energy levels

It calms the nerves and strengthens muscles

It nourishes the skin

It soothes arthritis

It combats insomnia

It helps soothe pile

It relieves fever and feverish conditions.

Really, biter leaf is loaded with medicinal health benefits. Drink bitter leaf juice and feel good. It is God's creation meant for you.

GRAPES

Grapes are a type of fruit that grow in clusters of 15 to 300. They come in various colours-crimson, black, dark blue, purple and green. Grapes are sweet, juicy with embodiment of simplicity in consumption. Just pluck and pop in your mouth. You don't need any cutting or peeling. This is good side of grapes.

WHY DO YOU NEED SOME GRAPES TO EAT?

Grapes are one of the most delicious fruits ever, rich in vitamins A, C, and B6. They have essential minerals like potassium, calcium, iron, phosphorus, magnesium and selenium.

Grapes are used for making edibles such as jelly, jam, juices, vinegar raisins and edible oil. Dried grapes are called raisins, sultanes, or currants and can be found in cakes and other confectionery.

Grape has a therapeutic value; it increases the moisture present in the lungs.

Grapes increase the nitric oxide levels in the blood, which prevent blood clots thereby reducing the chances of heart attacks.

Ripe grape juice is an important home remedy for curing migraine it should be taken early in the morning, without mixing additional water.

Grapes are very effective in overcoming constipation.

Grapes relieve heat, cures indigestion and irritation of the stomach.

Research has it that purple coloured Concord grape juice helps in preventing breast cancer.

Grapes contain a compound which has the capacity to bring down cholesterol level.

GUAVA

Guava is an exotic, affordable, and seasonal fruit that has many health benefits. It comes in varieties of shapes and colours. Its skin could be smooth or rough. Generally, the outer layer is green and turns pale yellow as it ripens. Guava can be round or pear-shaped while it is either white or pink on the inside. The white variety is more popular as the seeds are very small and the fruit sweet. The pink variety has bigger seeds and is a little sour; Guava is delicious with distinct aroma.

Does Guava have benefits; the answer is yes of course.

Guava has high concentration of antioxidants, offering protection against cell damage, which ages the skin and causes cancer. It actually helps the body fight against free radicals responsible for cell damage.

Nutritionist says one guava contains 165mg of vitamin C, compared to 69mg in an orange.

Guava is believed to control blood pressure and cholesterol because of the presence of potassium in it.

Guava is a good source of carbohydrate, vitamin A, vitamin B, iron, calcium and phosphorus

Guava fruit treats the gums, care for the teeth.

Guava can prevent dandruff when applied to the scalp.

Extracts from guava contain essential fatty acids that make the skin feel velvet.

Natural vitamin E present in guava smoothen our wrinkles. White guava pulp reduces stretch marks and repairs the skin around the eyes.

The leaves of guava have been found to be a rich source of tea used for treating cough and flu.
Guava can be included in a salad menu

All well said of guava, there is this negative feeling about guava. Many people believe that guava seeds can cause appendicitis, which is the reason they have struck off their menu list for good. But writing on the consumer line blog Ching Alano, says it is only a health myth.

Hear her, "It's a great urban legend that you must have been warned about by your grandmother. Tomato or guava seeds will not cause an inflamed appendix. The appendix gets infected when fecal matter or hardened mucus is obstructed in the opening of the appendix"

HAVE HEALTHY ROMANCE WITH FRUIT JUICE

If you are not fasting, after a cup of water intake in the home should be fresh fruit juice. Do you care for fruit juice? is a good question. Good answer should be, "Fine, I love it, but natural juice is good for me" The fact remains, packaged or canned juices are often saturated with chemicals. When you go for juice, let it be natural fruit juice, in the like of orange juice, pineapple juice or mango juice, guava juice etc.

ORANGE JUICE: The major nutritional content in oranges is vitamin C. it contains iron, and strengthens the immune system. Orange juice contains calcium and magnesium for strong teeth, healthy blood pressure level and healthy muscle function. The niacin in oranges helps maintain a healthy DNA and metabolizes food into energy.

Orange juice is rich in potassium, which is required to maintain a healthy cardiovascular system.

A daily glass of orange can also help prevent the recurrence of kidney stones and the fibre reduces the cholesterol level in the body. The natural sugar, fructose controls rising blood sugar level after meal.

A moderate size sweet orange contains 16g of carbohydrate that has 70 calories. These are important of energy source to the body, especially to the brain.

PINEAPPLE JUICE: Raw pineapple juice stimulates the kidney, relieves intestinal disorders and relieves intestinal worms.

Pineapple juice reduces excess water build-ups, thereby maintaining a healthy water balance in the body and helping to reduce weight.

The juice contains enzymes called bromeliad, which is helpful in healing athletic injuries, arthritis and post-operative swelling, as well as hemorrhoids, colitis, sore throat and menstrual disorders.

Raw pineapple juice is good for the heart as it reduces blood clots in the blood-stream; as a result 200-250ml of raw pineapple juice is suggested for daily intake.

MANGO JUICE: Mango juice has properties to destroy viruses. Enzymes in raw mangoes improve digestion. Eating the fruit helps relieve clogged pores in the skin.

Mango is a good source of the soluble fiber pectin, which slows sugar absorption.

LET YOUR FOOD BE PLANT BASED DIET

Plant based food comprises vegetables like lettuce, cabbage, spinach, peas and fruits. There are lots of advantage eating plant based diets.

The fact is, you live longer; about seven years longer when you eat plant based diet. You are 40per cent less likely to die from cancer and 20per cent less likely to die of heart related diseases because fruits and vegetables are full of antioxidant nutrients that protect the heart and its arteries.

People that eat plant based diet are slimmer than those who eat red meat. This is because diets that are higher in vegetable proteins are much lower in fat and calories. It is unlikely to fall victim to weight-related disorders such as stroke and diabetes.

The high water content in fruit cleanses the system Fruits counteract the acids in the system.

The five essentials of life that must come from foods-carbohydrates, minerals, vitamins, amino acids, and fatty acid are found in the fruit.

Fruits and vegetables are effective and efficient tool for weight loss

Fruit are predigested. Energy that would have otherwise been used for digestion is available for the body use.

Vegetables keep diabetes away. Vegetables have very little carbohydrate in them and very little impact on blood glucose that may encourage diabetes.
Eating vegetables regulate blood clotting. Most green vegetables contain minerals including iron, calcium, potassium, and magnesium as well as vitamin K, C, E and many of the B vitamins. Vitamin K alone can help regulate blood clotting

Above all, there are **secrets that abound in consuming fruits**. You should imbibe the principle of proper fruit consumption in your diet. The benefits enumerated above can be lost by consuming fruit, at the wrong time or in the wrong state. Take to these clues.

Remember to eat your fruit on an empty stomach

Eat your fruit 20-30 minutes before consuming any other food. This allows for the fruit or juice to leave your stomach. Some fruits take less time. Bananas and dried fruit need 40-60 minutes.

I presume the best time is, take it first in the morning mostly when you are not fasting!

Fruit has to be fresh and uncooked

Fruit that has altered in any way by heat do not supply any nutrients; canned fruit pies, baked pineapples and apple crumb lovers should take note.

The fact is, proper fruit consumption, is one of the nature's secrets of beauty, energy, longevity, balanced weight, happiness and health.

Vegetable strengthens the immune system. A plate of green vegetable contains nutrients that protect cells from damage, improve immune function, and can help protect our eyes from age-related disease

Eating vegetables prevent cardiovascular disease. There is compelling evidence that a diet rich in vegetables can lower the risk of heart disease and stroke. The higher its daily intake, there is lower chance of developing this disease.

Eating vegetable is a very effective tool for lowering blood pressure. A high blood pressure person should eat more of vegetable.
Eating vegetables aid good vision. A diet rich in vegetables appears to reduce the chances of developing cataract or macular degeneration.

AVOID FRIED FOOD

If possible, it is advisable to avoid eating fried food. There is this mistaken belief that fried food are for the high in society. Many are married to eating fried chicken on fried potatoes; fried plantain on fried eggs, teamed with sausages; eating fried rice boasting fried chicken and fried beef.

But have you thought of how healthy it is eating all these fried foods? The reason is that the frying process adds tons of calories and fat grams to meals. Other facts are, it's so easy to over eat when you snack on unhealthy fried foods, leading to excessive weight gain, which then increases the level of cholesterol in the body. Also, it is on record some restaurants and chefs prepare fried foods using unhealthy artificial oils that contain Trans fats.

With fried foods, your cells accumulate toxic products and you age more rapidly. Fried foods contain a toxic and potentially cancer-causing chemical acryl amide. They are high in fat and salt content but low in fiber and calcium content therefore increasing the possibility of obesity and chronic disease.

If you love eating fried foods cut it way back- once in two weeks. When you fry, use saturated fats that are low in the essential fatty acids. They are safer in frying. Doing this will create gold and wealth in your life.

ESSENTIALS OF BREAKFAST

There is the popular saying, **"Eat like a king in the morning; eat like a chief in the afternoon, and eat like a beggar in the evening"** What this mean is, eat nutritiously in the morning, eat moderate in the afternoon, eat little for dinner. Don't overload your stomach when going to bed at night.

Breakfast is the most important meal of the day to promote health and healing. After eight hours of sleep, which is akin to fast, there is need to break the fast (breakfast) because the brain needs fuel, to kick start the day.

The morning meal supplies the fuel, which includes glucose, vitamins, minerals and other essential nutrients. Lacking a full complement of such nutrients on daily basis due to lack of breakfast can prevent production of neurotransmitters essential for controlling electrical signals in the brain. Not eating breakfast also means lack of dopamine, which is important for movement, memory etc.

Another effect is, the brain finds another source of fuel by activating an emergency system that pulls energy from muscles destroying muscle tissues in the process. This is a sort of in-built fire-brigade approach to keep the brain running. Skipping breakfast means running the brain on reserve fuel; and when the brain cells are not well nourished, the whole body suffers.

Eating breakfast is one thing to start the day warm and be healthy is another. **It is unhealthy to consume cold foods and drinks including water in the early hours of the day.** Eating cold foods or drinking cold water first thing in the morning can shock the body by contracting blood vessels and muscles, blocking blood flow and negatively influencing digestion. Cold foods and drinks are troublesome for the body because morning air temperature is still slow and our bodies are already in a contracted state. Therefore, to consume warm foods and drink water in the morning is highly essential for health and vitality.

Above all, this is not a preach against fasting and prayer. There are people who skip breakfast, only eat at 2:00pm. This is communication with God, the Perfect One. When you break eat balanced diet, including fruits. Fasting is a spiritual crusade to move closer to God, to destroy works of darkness and prepare you for spiritual advancement. Therefore, fast when you choose to do it, and or, when it is declared in your church. It will build you and not harm you. Enjoy the wonders of God!

STAY HEALTHY ON A FAST

Though fasting is a demonstration of faith or penitence, this exercise also comes with a lot of benefits for your health. For one to be healthy, fasting plays major role. Fasting allows you lose weight. Obese can't find shade in fasting. You lose weight and keep fit.

A fast forces your body to dips into energy stores so as to get the fuel it needs to keep going which in turn keeps your digestive system at rest.

Fasting doesn't last forever. There must be a day you break. The question is what is the effective way to wake the body without overloading it, especially during a long period of fast?

Eat small amounts of raw fruits and vegetables for the few days, in the case of long fast, fruits and vegetable will allow the body to gently wake up the digestive system. Once you have eaten, wait till you feel hungry.
When you break, don't overload your digestive system with carbohydrates or heavy foods. It causes depression and sluggishness for the first few days of breaking a fast. Gradually increase the amount of raw fruits and vegetables in your diet.

To find gold and wealth in your fast, eat at the right time. God bless you. Amen.

POOR DIET

It is pathetic and sad to see how many homes feed this day. Many blame it on economic situation while those who are rich don't feed as expected. For example, in Nigeria our stable food constant is starch through the day. Morning menu rice (starch), afternoon Eba, a powdered food derived from cassava, is starch; at night it is either Semovita for the rich, or Amala, both are starch;

they are powdered substance derived from cassava or yam. The menus don't change the following day, except beans are eaten with Gari, a starchy powdered substance derived from cassava. Sad enough, meat hardly goes with the food, and where meat is eaten, it is as if in the midst of tense war, where meat is a scarce commodity.

Brethren, eat well, dress well, exercise well, sleep well, and rest well. A healthy body will be your best tool in reaching for success. You will be more energetic not only physically, but mentally as well. God rested on the seventh day after creation. Make time out for relaxation, going on vacation with your family will be a boost.

Thank you, may God bless you. Amen.

PRAYER POINTS

1. My mouth shall not be a trap of death in the name of Jesus

2. Hunger for food that will kill me before my time expire in the name of Jesus

3. Dark caterers assign to feed me in the dream die in the name of Jesus

4. Every altar of darkness dedicated to feed me catch fire and roast to ashes in the name of Jesus

5. Spirit of paralysis in my life, die in the name of Jesus

6. Satanic prophecy against my health, backfire in the name of Jesus

7. My heart receive divine deliverance and healing in the name of Jesus

8. My mouth shall not send me to untimely grave in the name of Jesus

9. Anything I took or ate but is now eating up my liver, I rebuke you expire in the name of Jesus

10. Arrow of cancer in my body come out by fire in the name of Jesus

11. I shall not suffer or die as a result of high blood pressure in the name of Jesus

12. Lord Jesus flush out toxins in my body in the name of Jesus

PRAYER TO SILENCE FINANCIAL CRISES

13. Every sickness in my eyes, receive healing and good health in the name of Jesus

14. I shall experience divine healing and good health in the name of Jesus.

15. Lord Jesus, cleanse my system with your blood in the name of Jesus.

16. I shall not suffer heart disease in the name of Jesus

17. Lord Jesus, provide me with money to feed well in the name of Jesus.

18. Skin disease, I speak against you disappear in the name of Jesus.

19. Arrow of arthritis fired against me; backfire in the name of Jesus.

20. Throat disease in my life; die in the name of Jesus.

21. Spirit of poverty die in the name of Jesus

22. Every serpent and scorpion programmed into my life die in the name of Jesus

23. Foundational problem in my life die in the name of Jesus

24. Covenant with sudden death, break in the name of Jesus

25. Pharaoh's cucumber shall not hold me captive in the name of Jesus

26. Pharaoh's melon shall not enslave me in the name of Jesus

27. Pharaoh's leeks shall not put me in bondage in the name of Jesus

28. Pharaoh's onions shall not turn me to servant in the name of Jesus

29. Pharaoh's garlic shall not kill me in the name of Jesus

30. Poisons as a result of the food I ate die in the name of Jesus

PRAYER TO SILENCE FINANCIAL CRISES

31. Supernatural energy locate me by fire in the name of Jesus

32. Every contamination in my life as a result of foods I ate, fire of God burn them to ashes in the name of Jesus.

YOU HAVE BATTLES TO WIN TRY THESE BOOKS

1. COMMAND THE DAY

Each day of the week is loaded with meanings and divine assurance. God did not create each day of the week for the fun of it. Blessings, success, gifts, resources, hopes, portfolios, duties, rights, prophecies, warnings and challenges, are loaded in each day.

Do you know the language, command or decree you can use to claim what belongs to you in each day of the week? Do you know in Christendom; Monday can be equated to one of the days of creation in Genesis chapter one? Do you know creation lasted for six days and God rested on the seventh day? What day of the week can Christian equate as the first day of the week, if we follow Christian calendar? What day can we call day seven?

This book shall give insight to these questions. It shall explain how you can command each day of the week according to creation in the book of Genesis chapter one.

Above all, you shall exercise your right and claim what is hidden in each day of the week.
Check for this in **COMMAND THE DAY.**

2. PRAYER TO REMEMBER DREAMS

A lot of people are passing through this spiritual epidemic on a daily basis. Their dream life is epileptic, having no ability to remember all dreams they dream, or sometimes forget everything entirely. This is nothing but spiritual havoc you need to erase from your spiritual record.

The answer to every form of spiritual blackout caused by spiritual erasers is found in, **PRAYER TO REMEMBER DREAMS.**

3.100% CONFESSSIONS AND PROPHECIES TO LOCATE HELPERS.

This is a wonderful book on confessions and prophecies to locate helpers and helpers to locate you. It is a prayer book loaded with over two thousand (2,000) prayer points.

The book unravels how to locate unknown helpers, prayers to arrest mind of helpers and prayers for manifestation after encounter with helpers.

4. ANOINTING FOR ELEVENTH HOUR HELP.

This book tells much of what to do at injury hour called eleventh hour. When you read and use this book as prescribed fear shall vanish in your life when pursuing a project, career or contract.

5. PRAYER TO LOCATE HELPERS.

Our divine helper is God. He created us to be together and be of help to one another. In the midst of no help we lost out, ending our journey in the wilderness.

There are keys assign to open right doors of life. You need right key to locate your helpers. Enough is enough; of suffering in silence.
With this book, you shall locate your helpers while your helpers shall locate you.

6. FIRE FOR FIRE PRAYER BOOK

This prayer book is fast at answering spiritual problems. It is a bulldozer prayer book, full of prayers all through. It is highly recommended for night vigil. Testimonies are pouring in daily from users of this book across the world!

7. PRAYER FOR THE FRUIT OF THE WOMB

This prayer book is children magnet. By faith and believe in God Almighty, as soon as you use this book open doors to child bearing shall be yours. Amen

8. PRAYER FOR PREGNANT WOMEN.

This is a spiritual prayer book loaded with prayers of solution for pregnant women. As soon as you take in, the prayers you shall pray from day one of conception to the day of delivery are written in this book.

9. WARFARE IN THE OFFICE

It is high time you pray prayers of power must change hands in office. Use this book and liberate yourself from every form of office yoke.

10. MY MARRIAGE SHALL NOT BREAK

Marriage is corner piece of life, happiness and joy. You need to hold it tight and guide it from wicked intruders and destroyer of homes.

11. VICTORY OVER SATANIC HOUSE

Are you a tenant, Land lord bombarded left and right, front and back by wicked people around you?

With this book you shall be liberated from the hooks of the enemy.

12. DICTIONARY OF DREAMS

This is a must book for every home. It gives accurate details to about **10,000 (Ten thousand) dreams and interpretations,** written in alphabetical order for quick reference and easy digestion. The book portrays spiritual revelations with sound prophetic guidelines. It is loaded with Biblical references and violent prayers.

Ask for yours today.

For Further Enquiries Contact
THE AUTHOR
EVANGELIST TELLA OLAYERI
P.O. Box 1872 Shomolu Lagos.
Tel: 08023583168

FROM AUTHOR'S DESK
BEFORE YOU GO

Hello,

Thank you for purchasing this book. Would you consider posting a review about this book? In addition to providing feedback and arousing others into Christ's bosom, reviews can help other customers to know about the book.

Please take a minute to leave a review on this book.

I would appreciate that!

Thank you in advance, for your review and your patronage!!

NOTE: You can get all my books from my website www.tellaolayeri.com

GOOD NEWS!!!

My audiobook is now available. To get one go to acx.com and search **Tella Olayeri**.

Thanks.

www.ingramcontent.com/pod-product-compliance
Lightning Source LLC
Chambersburg PA
CBHW052358220526
45465CB00003BB/1154